**Second Edition**

# World Link

## Developing English Fluency

**Susan Stempleski**
Nancy Douglas
James R. Morgan

# 2A
## Combo Split

HEINLE
CENGAGE Learning

Australia • Brazil • Japan • Korea • Mexico • Singapore • Spain • United Kingdom • United States

**World Link Combo Split 2A: Developing English Fluency**
**2nd Edition**

Susan Stempleski
Nancy Douglas
James R. Morgan

Publisher: Sherrise Roehr
Senior Development Editor:
Jennifer Meldrum
Senior Development Editor:
Katherine Carroll
Director of Global Marketing:
Ian Martin
Senior Product Marketing Manager:
Katie Kelley
Assistant Marketing Manager:
Anders Bylund
Content Project Manager:
John Sarantakis
Senior Print Buyer:
Mary Beth Hennebury
Composition: Bill Smith Group
Cover/Text Design: Page2 LLC
Cover Image: iStockphoto

Combo Split:
ISBN-13: 978-1-111-21933-8
ISBN-10: 1-111-21933-8

Combo Split with Student CD-ROM:
ISBN-13: 978-1-4240-6686-5
ISBN-10: 1-4240-6686-7

**Heinle**
20 Channel Center Street
Boston, MA 02210
USA

Cengage learning is a leading provider of customized learning solutions with office locations around the globe, including Singapore, the United Kingdom, Australia, Mexico, Brazil, and Japan. Locate our local office at:
**international.cengage.com/region**

Cengage Learning products are represented in Canada by Nelson Education, Ltd.

Visit Heinle online at **elt.heinle.com**
Visit our corporate website at **cengage.com**

Printed in the United States of America
1 2 3 4 5 6 7 8 9 10 - 14 13 12 11 10

# Acknowledgments

Thank you to the educators who provided invaluable feedback throughout the development of the second edition of the *World Link* series: Rocio Abarca, Instituto Tecnológico de Costa Rica / FUNDATEC; Anthony Acevedo, ICPNA (Instituto Cultural Peruano Norteamericano); David Aduviri, CBA (Centro Boliviano Americano) - La Paz; Ramon Aguilar, Universidad Tecnológica de Hermosillo; Miguel Arrazola, CBA (Centro Boliviano Americano) - Santa Cruz; Cecilia Avila, Universidad de Xalapa; Isabel Baracat, CCI (Centro de Comunicação Inglesa); Andrea Brotto, CEICOM (Centro de Idiomas para Comunidades); George Bozanich, Soongsil University; Emma Campo, Universidad Central; Martha Carrasco, Universidad Autonoma de Sinaloa; Herbert Chavel, Korea Advanced Institute of Science and Technology; Denise de Bartolomeo, AMICANA (Asociación Mendocina de Intercambio Cultural Argentino Norteamericano); Rodrigo de Campos Rezende, SEVEN Idiomas; John Dennis, Hokuriku University; Kirvin Andrew Dyer, Yan Ping High School; Daniela Frillochi, ARICANA (Asociación Rosarina de Intercambio Cultural Argentino Norteamericano); Jose Gonzales, ICPNA (Instituto Cultural Peruano Norteamericano); Marina Gonzalez, Instituto Universitario de Lenguas Modernas; Robert Gordon, Korea Advanced Institute of Science and Technology; Gu Yingruo, Research Institute of Xiangzhou District, ZhuHai; Yo-Tien Ho, Takming University; Roxana Jimenez, Instituto Tecnológico de Costa Rica / FUNDATEC; Sirina Kainongsuang, Perfect Publishing Company Limited; Karen Ko, ChinYi University; Ching-Hua Lin, National Taiwan University of Science and Technology; Simon Liu, ChinYi University; Maria Helena Luna, Tronwell; Ady Marrero, Alianza Cultural Uruguay Estados Unidos; Nancy Mcaleer, ELC Universidad Interamericana de Panama; Michael McCallister, Feng Chia University Language Center; José Antonio Mendes Lopes, ICBEU (Instituto Cultural Brasil Estados Unidos); Leonardo Mercado, ICPNA (Instituto Cultural Peruano Norteamericano); Tania Molina, Instituto Tecnológico de Costa Rica / FUNDATEC; Iliana Mora, Instituto Tecnológico de Costa Rica / FUNDATEC; Fernando Morales, Universidad Tecnológica de Hermosillo; Vivian Morghen, ICANA (Instituto Cultural Argentino Norteamericano); Niu Yuchun, New Oriental School Beijing; Elizabeth Ortiz, COPEI (Copol English Institute); Virginia Ortiz, Universidad Autonoma de Tamaulipas; Peter Reilly, Universidad Bonaterra; Ren Huijun, New Oriental School Hangzhou; Andreina Romero, URBE (Universidad Rafael Belloso Chacín); Adelina Ruiz, Instituto Tecnologico de Estudios Superiores de Occidente; Eleonora Salas, IICANA (Instituto de Intercambio Cultural Argentino Norteamericano); Mary Sarawit, Naresuan University International College; Jenay Seymour, Hong-ik University; Huang Shuang, Shanghai International Studies University; Sávio Siqueira, ACBEU (Asociação Cultural Brasil Estados Unidos) / UFBA (Universidade Federal da Bahia); Beatriz Solina, ARICANA (Asociación Rosarina de Intercambio Cultural Argentino Norteamericano); Tran Nguyen Hoai Chi, Vietnam USA Society English Training Service Center; Maria Inés Valsecchi, Universidad Nacional de Río Cuarto; Patricia Veciño, ICANA (Instituto Cultural Argentino Norteamericano); Punchalee Wasanasomsithi, Chulalongkorn University; Tomoe Watanabe, Hiroshima City University; Tomohiro Yanagi, Chubu University; Jia Yuan, Global IELTS School.

# Scope & Sequence

| Pronunciation | Speaking & Speaking Strategy | Reading | Writing | Communication |
|---|---|---|---|---|
| **Reduction of present continuous** *-ing* **ending** p. 3 | **I'd like you to meet . . .** p. 4 <br> Introducing a person <br> Responding to introductions | **A book of memories** p. 8 <br> Skim for the main idea <br> Summarize a text | **The first day of class** p. 11 <br> Write about a time you attended a class for the first time | * **Is it you?** p. 6 <br> Guessing classmates' identities based on their habits <br><br> * **Class awards** p. 11 <br> Selecting classmates to receive different awards |
| **Sentence stress and rhythm** p. 13 | **How about Thai food?** p. 14 <br> Making and responding to suggestions | **The healthiest people in the world** p. 18 <br> Use the title and photo to make predictions <br> Scan to find information and complete a chart | **Restaurant review** p. 21 <br> Write a review of a restaurant you know | * **Veronica's Restaurant** p. 16 <br> Creating a radio advertisement for an improved restaurant <br><br> * **Comparing foods** p. 21 <br> Creating a menu for a new restaurant |
| **Past tense vowel shifts** p. 23 | **I bet she's good at math.** p. 24 <br> Talking about possibility | **Mysterious artwork** p. 28 <br> Use photos to make predictions <br> Identify main ideas in paragraphs | **A strange event** p. 30 <br> Write your own ending to a story | * **Strange but true stories** p. 26 <br> Retelling a story and discussing possibilities <br><br> * **What's your theory?** p. 31 <br> Discussing theories of unsolved world mysteries |
| **Unstressed** *of* **in rapid speech** p. 37 | **I know what you're saying, but . . .** p. 38 <br> Disagreeing | **Trendspotting** p.42 <br> Make predictions <br> Understand text organization <br> Draw conclusions | **What's your advice?** p. 45 <br> Write a letter requesting advice | * **What should they do?** p. 40 <br> Giving an opinion about what a person should do <br><br> * **Do you need a makeover?** p. 45 <br> Using a survey to determine your partner's trendiness |
| **Reduced forms of** *could you* **and** *would you* p. 47 | **I'd like to make an appointment.** p. 48 <br> Making appointments | **Surprising neighborhoods** p. 52 <br> Use photos to make predictions <br> Categorize information | **Come to my neighborhood** p. 54 <br> Write about your neighborhood | * **My** *benriya* **service** p. 50 <br> Creating an errand/chore service <br><br> * **Improving your community** p. 55 <br> Proposing a plan to make your community a better place |
| **Reduced pronunciation of** *going to* p. 57 | **Look on the bright side.** p. 58 <br> Offering another point of view | **An opportunity of a lifetime** p. 62 <br> Make and check predictions <br> Guess the meaning of words from context | **My life now and in the future** p. 65 <br> Write predictions about your future | * **Find someone who . . .** p. 60 <br> Talking to people about their plans for the future <br><br> * **Predicting the future** p. 65 <br> Using a profile to make predictions about someone's future |

## 1  Vocabulary Link    How do you know each other?

**A**  Mario is talking about four people in his life. How does he know each person? Tell a partner.

Cintra

> Cintra and I went out in the past, but she's not my girlfriend anymore. We're just friends now.

> I met Tomas and Silvia in college. We attended the same school. They both live in different cities now, but we're still close friends.

> Adrian and I work together. He's a nice guy, but to be honest, he's just an acquaintance. I don't know him very well.

Adrian

Mario

Tomas

Silvia

**B**  In **A**, find a word or phrase in blue that has a similar meaning to each underlined word or phrase in the sentences in the chart. Write the word or phrase on the line. Compare your answers with a partner.

| Words used to talk about ... | | |
|---|---|---|
| **friends** | **workmates** | **classmates** |
| 1. Cintra and I <u>dated</u> in the past.  <br> _went out_ | 5. We're <u>coworkers</u>.  <br> _____ | 6. We <u>went to</u> the same school.  <br> _____ |
| 2. He's <u>someone I know, but not very well</u>.  _____ | | |
| 3. We're <u>not dating</u> now.  <br> _____ | | |
| 4. We're still <u>good friends</u>.  <br> _____ | | |

**C**  Make a list of three people you know and then show your list to a partner. Tell your partner two facts about each person on your list.

> So, who is Yoon?

> He's a good friend. We went to high school together.

## 2 Listening How do you know Michael?

 **A** Look at the pictures below. How do you think the people in each picture know each other? Tell a partner.

 **B** Listen to the conversations and number the pictures in **A** in the order (1, 2, 3) you hear them. One picture is extra.

CD 1
Track 2

 **C** Look at your answers (1, 2, 3) in **B** and listen again. Which sentence is true about the people in each photo? Circle the correct answer.

CD 1
Track 2

1. a. They're dating.          b. They're acquaintances.     c. They're just friends.

2. a. They went to the same school.     b. They're just friends.     c. They're coworkers.

3. a. They're in the same class.     b. They're acquaintances.     c. They're close friends.

 **D** Look again at the pictures in **A**. Who are the people? How do they know each other? Tell a partner.

## 3 Pronunciation  Reduction of present continuous *-ing* ending

 **A** Listen to the conversations. Notice how the underlined verbs are pronounced. Then practice with a partner.

CD 1
Track 3

1. **Clara:** Now I remember you. How are you <u>doing</u>?

   **Rakesh:** Fine. How about you?

2. **Lisa:** Hey, Josh. Are you busy?

   **Josh:** Yeah. I'm <u>writing</u> a paper for my English class.

   **Lisa:** OK. Talk to you later.

 **B** Practice reading the sentences below with a partner. Use the reduced pronunciation of *-ing*.

1. I'm trying to finish my homework.     3. She's working in her garden.

2. I'm fixing my car.     4. We're going to the movies.

 **C** Now listen and check your pronunciation.

CD 1
Track 4

# 4 Speaking    **I'd like you to meet . . .**

**A**   Listen to the conversations. Who is meeting for the first time?

**Conversation 1**

| | |
|---|---|
| Maria: | Hi, Junko. |
| Junko: | Hi, Maria. It's good to see you again! How are you? |
| Maria: | Fine. How about you? |
| Junko: | Pretty good. |
| Maria: | Oh, and this is my friend Ricardo. We both go to City University. |
| Junko: | Hey, Ricardo. Nice to meet you. |
| Ricardo: | Yeah, you too. |

**Conversation 2**

| | |
|---|---|
| Mr. Otani: | Morning, Miriam. |
| Miriam: | Good morning, Mr. Otani. . . . Oh, Mr. Otani, I'd like you to meet Andres Garcia. He started working here yesterday. Andres, Mr. Otani is our V.P. of Sales. |
| Mr. Otani: | Nice to meet you, Andres. |
| Andres: | It's very nice to meet you, too, Mr. Otani. |

**ASK ANSWER**

What does Maria say to introduce Ricardo?
What does Miriam say to introduce Andres?

**B**   Practice both conversations with two partners.

# 5 Speaking Strategy

**A**   Work in groups of three: Student A, Student B, and Student C.

1. Student A: Choose a famous person to be. Write down your identity on a piece of paper and give it to Student B.

2. Student B: Read the identity of Student A. Then introduce Student A to Student C formally.

3. Change roles and follow steps 1 and 2 again.

| Useful Expressions | | |
|---|---|---|
| | **Introducing a person to someone else** | **Responding to introductions** |
| formal | Mr. Otani, **I'd like to introduce you to** Andres. | It's (very) nice to meet you. (It's) nice / good to meet you, too. |
| | Mr. Otani, **I'd like you to meet** Andres. | |
| | Junko, **this is** Ricardo. Junko, **meet** Ricardo. | Nice / Good to meet you. You, too. |
| informal | Junko, Ricardo. | |

**B**   Now introduce the "famous friends" you met in **A** to your other classmates. Use a formal or informal style.

Ana, I'd like you to meet
_____.
(name)

It's nice to meet you,
_____.
(name)

It's nice to meet you too, Ana.

# 6 Language Link   The simple present vs. the present continuous

**A**   Look at the pictures and read about Diane. Then use the words in the box to complete sentences 1, 2, and 3 below.

> fact   right now   routine   temporary

Diane **works** in the sales department. She always **arrives** at work at 8:00 a.m.

Diane **is talking** on the telephone. She **is** also **typing** a report.

They need help in the finance department. Diane **is working** there this week only.

1. Sentence 1 states a general _____. Sentence 2 talks about a habit or _____. Use the simple present.

2. These events are happening _____. Use the present continuous.

3. This is a _____ situation. Use the present continuous.

**B**   Veronique Lesarg is a doctor. Use the simple present or present continuous to complete her profile.

My name (1) _____ (be) Veronique Lesarg. I (2) _____ (live) in Montreal. I (3) _____ (be) a pediatrician, a doctor for children. I usually (4) _____ (work) in a hospital, but these days, I (5) _____ (volunteer) for an organization called *Doctors Without Borders*. They (6) _____ (send) staff to other countries. This year, I (7) _____ (work) in Africa. At the moment, I (8) _____ (write) to you from a small village. There's no hospital here, so right now we (9) _____ (build) one.

> **Time expressions and the present continuous**
>
> Find and circle the three other time expressions used with the present continuous in the profile.

**C**   Complete these sentences to make questions in the simple present or the present continuous. Use the verbs in the box.

> do   eat   have   study   take   talk

**1. A:** Why ___*are you studying*___ English ?
   **B:** I need it for my work.

**2. A:** _____ any other classes this term?
   **B:** Yes, I am—two business classes.

**3. A:** When _____ breakfast?
   **B:** About 7:00, usually.

**4. A:** How many brothers and sisters _____?
   **B:** Four brothers and one sister.

**5. A:** What _____ on the weekends?
   **B:** Play golf. And relax.

**6. A:** Who _____ to right now?
   **B:** Alex.

**D**   Now take turns asking and answering the questions in **C** with a partner.

## 7 Communication   Is it you?

**A**   Take a sheet of paper and cut it into five strips.
On strips 1-3, write the following:

  1. a routine you never change

  2. an unusual habit

  3. a general fact about yourself

Continue your list.
On strips 4 and 5, write the following:

  4. an activity you are doing these days

  5. why you are studying English

*1. I always get up at 5 a.m.*

*2. I sometimes eat peanut butter and tomato sandwiches.*

*3. I have a twin brother.*

*4. I'm learning to play the guitar.*

*5. I'm studying English because it's my major.*

**B**   Give your papers to the teacher. Your teacher
will mix up the papers and give you five new sentences.

**C**   Talk to your classmates.
Ask questions to find out who wrote each sentence.

**D**   Tell the class an interesting fact you learned about one of your classmates.

# All About Me

## Lesson B   School days

## 1   Vocabulary Link   I'm taking a class.

 **A**   Read the statements and match each person with his or her picture below.
Then ask a partner: What is each person doing? Why?

1. "My parents think playing sports is important. So, after school, I have soccer practice every day. I also take tennis lessons for an hour on the weekend."

2. "I'm taking a class to prepare for the university entrance exam. The class meets for three hours a day. It's a lot of work, but I need help to pass the test."

3. "Two months ago, I was failing math—getting D's and F's. Now a tutor comes to my house and helps me with my homework, and I'm finally getting a good grade in the class!"

**B**   Complete the sentences with the correct form of the blue word(s) in **A**.

1. I can't go to the movies with you. I _____ baseball _____ this afternoon.

2. Tyler never studies, so now he is _____ a bad _____ in all his classes.

3. Maiko studied really hard and she _____ the test!

4. This term, I'm _____ two business classes at City University.

5. Our English class _____ on Tuesdays and Thursdays.

6. To _____ for tomorrow's class, please read pages 20 to 45.

7. My piano _____ is only for 30 minutes. After that, we can go to the store.

8. Liam _____ his biology class, so he has to retake it next term.

9. Nico is a _____ . He helps children with their homework.

> **ASK   ANSWER**
> 1. How are you doing in school? Do you get good grades?
> 2. Are you taking any special classes or lessons now (or did you in the past)? If yes, why? How often do (or did) the classes meet?

## 2 Listening    GBL Learning Center

**A**    Look at the places listed below. Why do people go to these places? What do they learn? Discuss your ideas with a partner.

> a language institute        a sports camp        a test preparation center

CD 1
Track 6

**B**    You are going to hear a radio ad. Listen. Which place in **A** is the ad talking about? What does the place help people do?

CD 1
Track 7

**C**    Listen to the rest of the radio ad. Match each person to his or her job and his or her results. Some answers are extra. One answer is used two times.

1.

2.

a. doctor

b. engineer

c. soccer player

d. student


e. score went up 50 points

f. score went up 15 points

g. passed the first time

3.

h. failed and then passed

ASK ANSWER

Think about the three people in the listening and their results. What do you think they are doing now?

## 3 Reading    A book of memories

**A**    Skim the reading on page 9. Look quickly at the title, photo, and the first and last sentence in each paragraph. Then complete the sentence below.

A yearbook is _____ for a certain school year.

a. a list of the most popular students

b. a book used to prepare for exams

c. a collection of student photos and activities

d. a record of students' grades

**B** Read the article and check your answer in **A**.

# Yearbooks in the United States

Most high schools in the United States publish a yearbook once a year, usually in the spring. It is a record of the school year—a "book of memories" for the students.

Inside a yearbook is each student's photo. The seniors are graduating soon, and their photos appear first. Next are the juniors. They are one year behind the seniors. Then come the sophomores, or second-year students. The last photos are the first-year students, the freshmen. The yearbook is not only about students. The teachers have photos, too.

The yearbook also has photos and descriptions of sports teams, academic subjects, and extracurricular activities. These are activities students do after school, such as the chess club and Spanish club. There is even a yearbook club. Students in this club write, design, and take photos all year for the yearbook. At the end of the year, the book is printed.

In the yearbook, some students receive special titles. The seniors vote and choose the "class clown" (a funny student), the "most likely to succeed" (a student who got the best grades), and the "best dressed" (a student with a good fashion sense). There are also other awards and categories.

Students usually sign each other's yearbooks. This is especially important for the seniors because they are graduating. Students write notes to each other, such as, "We had a lot of fun," or "I'll never forget you." They also write about all the fun and funny experiences they shared in school together.

**C** Complete the following summary using words from the article in **B**. Compare your answers with a partner.

A yearbook is a (1) _____ of the school year. You will find each student's (2) _____ in a yearbook. Photos of the (3) _____ come first. The yearbook features (4) _____ teams, academic subjects, and extracurricular activities. There are many clubs: the (5) _____ club makes the yearbook. Seniors vote and give some students (6) _____ such as "class clown." Students (7) _____ their classmates' yearbooks. The yearbook is truly a book of (8) _____ .

**ASK** **ANSWER**

Did/Does your high school have a yearbook? If yes, what is it like?
If no, would you like to have one? What would you put in your school yearbook?

# 4 Language Link  Review of the simple past

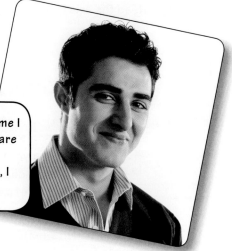

**A** Read about Diego's high school experiences. Underline the regular simple past verbs. Circle the irregular ones. Then tell a partner: what happened to Diego?

> In high school, I <u>studied</u> a lot and (got) good grades. But the first time I took the university entrance exam, I failed. That was hard. To prepare for the next exam, I went to a test prep center. Two good things happened there: I met my girlfriend in the class. And the next time, I passed the entrance exam!

**B** Look at the high school photos of these two famous people. Complete each profile with the correct past tense verbs from the box. Then fill in their names.

| act become die go take write |
| --- |

Her mother (1) _____ when she was six years old. In high school, she (2) _____ drama and dance classes. She (3) _____ to New York in 1977, and later she (4) _____ a very famous singer. She also (5) _____ books for children and (6) _____ in movies.

Her name is (7) _____ Louise Ciccone.

| be divorce enter move run win |
| --- |

He (1) _____ born in Hawaii to an American mother and a Kenyan father. His parents (2) _____ and later he (3) _____ with his family to Indonesia and then again to the U.S. In 1988, he (4) _____ Harvard Law School and in 2008, he (5) _____ for President of the United States. He (6) _____ .

His name is (7) _____ _____ .

**C** Choose a person in **B** and write 3 or 4 questions about him or her. Then ask your partner the questions.

> In high school, what classes did she take?

_____

_____

_____

_____

## 5 Writing    **The first day of class**

**A**  Think about your first day in English class. On a separate piece of paper, explain what happened on that day.

**B**  Exchange papers with a partner. Tell the class about your partner's memories.

*I remember our first English class. I didn't know anyone. I sat next to Anika. She was really nice. When the class started, the teacher asked me a question but I got nervous and couldn't answer. Later, we played a game and I talked a lot.*

## 6 Communication    **Class awards**

**A**  Work with a partner. Look at the awards below. Invent one more award for number 6.

1. Name: _____

2. Name:_____

3. Name:_____

4. Name:_____

5. Name:_____

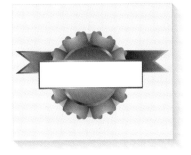

6. Name:_____

**B**  Who would be the best person in your class to receive each award in **A**? Write the names under the awards.

**C**  Tell the class your choices in **A**. Explain your reasons.

*We chose Carlos as the "friendliest." On the first day of class, he said "hello" to everyone. He also helped . . .*

Check out the World Link video.

Practice your English online at http://elt.heinle.com/worldlink

## 1  Vocabulary Link    Street foods

**A**  Read about these street foods. Which one(s) would you like to try? Why?

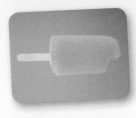

# Street Foods
## from around the World

*Are you hungry and looking for a fast, inexpensive, and tasty snack? Here are three traditional street foods from around the world.*

### Paletas (Mexico)

*What it is:* A popsicle, usually made with juice or water and pieces of fresh fruit. Sometimes, red chili pepper is also added to a paleta. It's the perfect mix of sweet and spicy flavors!

### Doner kebap (Turkey)

*What it is:* Pieces of juicy meat (usually lamb or chicken) served on a thin piece of bread with different sauces. It's delicious!

### Maeng da (Thailand)

*What it is:* Water beetles (a kind of insect) are fried in oil and then salt is added. The result: a salty snack that tastes like potato chips!

**Food • 27**

**-y** = "full of something":
salty, spicy, oily, healthy,

_____ , _____

**B**  Answer the questions below with a partner.

   1. Read the note above. Then find two other adjectives in **A** that end in *-y.*

   2. Choose four words from the note. Think of a matching food for each one.

**C**  What's your favorite street food? Tell your partner. Describe the food's taste.

> Near my house, you can buy churros on the street. They're fried pieces of dough with sugar added. They're sweet and delicious!

### Describing how something tastes

This soup **is** tasty/delicious/terrible/sweet/salty/spicy.

This tea **tastes** good/delicious/terrible/sweet/salty/spicy.

This meat **tastes like** chicken.

## 2 Listening   Foods of the southern United States

**A**   Look at the four photos below. What do you think each food tastes like? Tell your partner.

**B**   Listen to Bill and Marta's conversation. Complete the information about the food.

CD 1
Track 8

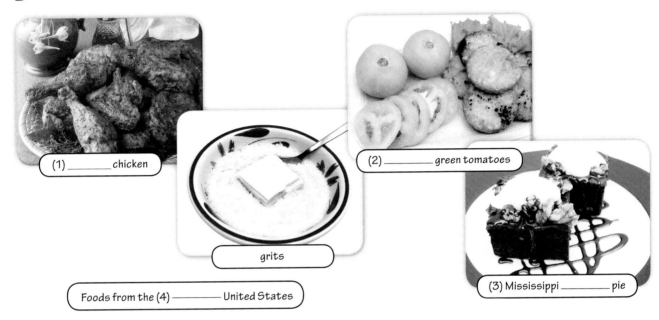

(1) _____ chicken

grits

(2) _____ green tomatoes

(3) Mississippi _____ pie

Foods from the (4) _____ United States

**C**   Listen to the rest of the conversation. Write the words used to describe the foods. Then circle the food Marta *didn't* like. Why didn't she like it?

CD 1
Track 9

1. The chicken was _____.

2. The grits tasted like oatmeal with a strong _____ flavor.

3. The tomatoes were _____, but they went _____ with the chicken and grits.

4. The dessert was a thick, _____ pie. It was too _____.

> **ASK  ANSWER**
>
> Do these four foods sound good to you? Why or why not?
> Is your hometown (or region) famous for a special food? Describe it.

## 3 Pronunciation   Sentence stress and rhythm

**A**   Listen and repeat the sentences. Note where the stress falls.

CD 1
Track 10

ORanges are SWEETer than GRAPEfruit.     PoTAto chips are SALtier than CRACKers.

**B**   Circle the stressed syllables in these sentences. Then listen and check your answers. Practice saying the sentences with a partner.

CD 1
Track 11

1. Math is harder than English.

2. Apples are juicier than carrots.

3. The curry is spicier than the chili.

4. January is colder than February.

## 4 Speaking    How about Thai food?

CD 1
Track 12

**A**   Listen to the conversation. Then answer the questions.

    1. What are Jose and Jill going to eat for dinner?

    2. How do Jose and Jill make suggestions? Underline the words.

**Jose:**   So, Jill, where do you want to go to dinner tonight?

**Jill:**     I don't know. Why don't we go to the pizza place on the corner?

**Jose:**   Pizza again? I don't really feel like it.

**Jill:**     OK, how about Thai food instead?

**Jose:**   Fine with me. Where do you want to go?

**Jill:**     Well, Thai House is near here. And there's another place — The Thai Cafe — but it's downtown.

**Jose:**   Thai House is closer. Let's go there.

**Jill:**     Sounds good!

**B**   Practice the conversation with a partner.

## 5 Speaking Strategy

**A**   Study the Useful Expressions. Then complete the dialogs below with a partner. Sometimes more than one answer is possible.

    **1. A:** _____ stop at that cafe for coffee.
       **B:** Sounds _____!

    **2. A:** What time do you want to meet in the morning?
       **B:** _____ meet at 7:00?
       **A:** That's a little early. _____ meeting at 8:00 instead?
       **B:** _____ with me. See you then.

    **3. A:** What do you want to do today?
       **B:** _____ going to the beach?
       **A:** I don't _____ it. _____ see a movie instead.
       **B:** OK, _____ good.

### Useful Expressions

| Making suggestions | | | Responding to suggestions |
|---|---|---|---|
| Statements | | | Great idea! |
| Let's | have | Thai food for dinner. | (That) sounds good (to me). |
| | | | Fine with me. |
| Questions | | | I don't really want to. |
| Why don't we | have | Thai food for dinner? | I don't really feel like it. |
| How / What about | having | | |

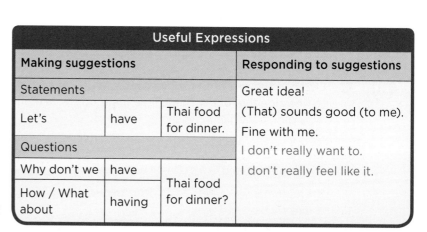

Why don't we go to Parr's Steakhouse for lunch?

That's a great idea!

I don't really feel like steak. How about having Indian food instead?

**B**   Get into a group of three and do the following.

    1. On your own: think of two restaurants that are good for a meal.

    2. Suggest one of the restaurants to your partners. They can accept or refuse. If a person refuses, he or she should say why and suggest another restaurant.

    3. Change roles and repeat steps 1 and 2.

## 6 Language Link  The comparative form of adjectives

**A**  Read the advertisement. Underline all the adjectives. Then tell a partner: How are the underlined adjectives similar? How are they different?

ANNOUNCING . . .

# GRAND REOPENING!!

JOE'S CHICKEN SHACK

Yes, we are open again! Come and see the improvements:
The portions were <u>large</u> . . .
but now they are **LARGER**!

Our spicy chicken is even **SPICIER**!
The seating area was spacious… but now it's **MORE SPACIOUS**!
Joe's Chicken Shack was good, but now it's **BETTER** than ever!

**B**  Complete the chart with the missing words. Then check your answers with a partner.

| The comparative form of adjectives | | | | | |
|---|---|---|---|---|---|
| **One syllable** | | **Two syllables** | | **Three or more syllables** | |
| _____ | sweeter | simple | _____ | _____ | more refreshing |
| large | _____ | _____ | spicier | delicious | _____ |
| big | bigger | _____ | more crowded | interesting | _____ |

*Notice!* The comparative form of *good* is *better*.

**C**  Complete the sentences with the comparative form of the adjective in parentheses.

1. The red curry is _____spicier_____ than the green curry. (spicy)

2. Cherry candy is _____ than real cherries. (sweet)

3. Wow! This apple pie is _____ than my Mom's! (delicious)

4. Our English teacher is _____ than our math teacher. (popular)

5. You're a _____ cook than I am. (good)

6. She is really embarrassed. Her face is _____ than an apple! (red)

*The comparative is often followed by* than *when comparing two things.*

**D**  Think of foods to compare using the adjectives in the box. Then say sentences comparing the foods with a partner.

> good   healthy   refreshing   salty   sweet

> *Apples are healthier than potato chips.*

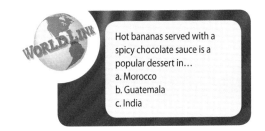

WORLD LINK

Hot bananas served with a spicy chocolate sauce is a popular dessert in…
a. Morocco
b. Guatemala
c. India

# 7 Communication   Veronica's Restaurant

**A**  Look at the pictures of Veronica's Restaurant. Talk about the changes you see. Use the adjectives in the box to help you.

| clean | new | happy |
|-------|-----|-------|
| bright | big | cheerful |
| messy | old | dirty |
| good | bad | nice |
| beautiful | | |

The old Veronica's

The old Veronica's was dirty. The new Veronica's is cleaner.

The new Veronica's

**B**  With a partner, make a fifteen-second radio advertisement for the new Veronica's using your ideas from **A**. Write your ideas below. Then practice saying the announcement aloud.

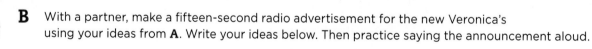

**C**  Present your radio advertisement to the class.
Whose was the best? Why?

Come and see the new Veronica's! It's bigger and better than ever!

# Let's Eat!

## Lesson B  Eating well

## 1  Vocabulary Link   What's their secret?

**A**   Read the article below. Then answer the questions with a partner.

1. How are the five countries in the article similar?

2. Why are these people's traditional diets special?

yourhealth*.com

# Your Health

Mexico, Japan, Cameroon, Iceland, and Greece. What do these five countries have in common? In her book, *The Jungle Effect*, Dr. Daphne Miller says these places have some of the healthiest people in the world.

What's their secret? Dr. Miller says these people's traditional diets have important health benefits. The things they eat and drink increase their energy, help them think better, and protect against dangerous diseases like cancer.

Dr. Miller says a healthy diet and lifestyle are important. She says we should…

- eat more green vegetables, fish, yogurt, corn, beans, and spices.
- cut back on red meat and processed* foods.
- eat out in restaurants less.
- eliminate unhealthy habits, like smoking.
- get plenty of exercise.

*__processed__: instant (pre-made)

**B**   Which statements would Dr. Miller agree with? Explain your answers to a partner.

1. People should eat more hamburgers.

2. Don't smoke.

3. Don't eat instant noodles too often.

4. Cook at home more.

5. Going to the gym once a month is enough.

6. Salmon, spinach, and black beans make up a healthy meal.

**C**   Discuss the questions with a partner.
Do you have a healthy diet and lifestyle? Why or why not?
How often do you eat or drink the things listed in the article?

**Word Partnership** *diet*
balanced/healthy/unhealthy/
strict/traditional **diet**

## 2 Listening — The Slow Food Movement

**A** Discuss the questions with a partner.

1. We often hear about "fast food" and "instant food." What is it?

2. How often do you eat it?

CD 1
Track 13

**B** You are going to hear two people talking about the Slow Food Movement.

1. Which statements below do you think its members believe?

2. Listen and circle the correct answer(s).

> A **movement** is a group of people who have the same beliefs or ideas.
>
> A **member** is a part of the group.

People should _____.

a. serve food slowly

b. eat no fast or instant foods

c. learn to prepare their own meals

d. grow food slowly and carefully

**C** Read the six statements below. Then listen again. For each sentence, choose *T* (true), *F* (false), or *NS* (not said). Explain your answer choices to a partner.

CD 1
Track 13

**Mr. Moretti thinks . . .**

| | | | |
|---|---|---|---|
| 1. most Slow Food members are Italian. | T | F | NS |
| 2. eating a slow food diet is difficult for busy people. | T | F | NS |
| 3. a slow food diet has many health benefits. | T | F | NS |
| 4. a slow food diet is good for the environment. | T | F | NS |
| 5. you should learn your grandparents' recipes. | T | F | NS |
| 6. more stores are selling slow food items these days. | T | F | NS |

**ASK ANSWER**

Would you join the Slow Food Movement? Why or why not?

## 3 Reading — The healthiest people in the world

**A** Look quickly at the title, picture, and reading on page 19.
Then try to guess the answers to 1 and 2 below. Explain your ideas to a partner.

1. The reading is mainly about _____.

a. people from around the world

b. healthcare for older people

c. a group of people from Japan

d. older people in the United States

2. What is unusual about these people?

a. Most of them are women.

b. A large number live to age 100 or older.

c. They have the spiciest food in the world.

d. There are only 100 of them in the world.

**B** Now read the article and check your answers to 1 and 2 in **A**.

# The Healthiest Lifestyle in the World?

In many countries around the world, people are living longer than before. People have healthier lifestyles, and healthcare is better, too.

Okinawa is an island off the coast of Japan. The people on Okinawa, the Okinawans, may have the longest lives and healthiest lifestyles in the world.

Researchers did a study. They started by looking at city and town birth records from 1879. They didn't expect to find many centenarians (hundred-year-olds) in the records, so they were very surprised to find so many old and healthy people living in Okinawa. The United States, for example, has 10 centenarians per 100,000 people. In Okinawa there are 34 centenarians per 100,000 people!

What is the Okinawans' secret? First, they eat a healthy diet that includes fresh fruits and vegetables. They also eat fish often and drink plenty of water and green tea. But researchers think that the Okinawans have other healthy habits as well. They don't do hard exercise such as weight lifting or jogging. Instead, they prefer relaxing activities like gardening and walking. Researchers say that older Okinawans also have a good attitude[1] about aging. They sit quietly and relax their minds with deep breathing exercises. They also enjoy massage.

[1] **attitude:** the way you think or feel about something

**C** Scan the article and complete the chart below. You have two minutes.

### Okinawan Centenarians

| What they eat | What they drink |
|---|---|
| _____ | _____ |
| _____ | _____ |
| **How they exercise** | **How they relax** |
| _____ | _____ |
| _____ | _____ |

Why do Okinawans live so long? Give some reasons.
Do people in your country have healthy lifestyles? Give examples.

## 4 Language Link   The superlative form of adjectives

**A**   Read the information about the restaurants. Then complete the sentences below with the correct form of each adjective.

opened: 1942
dinner menu: 40 euros

opened: 1925
dinner menu: 60 euros

opened: 1886
dinner menu: 80 euros

Restaurant A is _____old_____.

Restaurant B is _____than Restaurant A.

Restaurant C is **the oldest** restaurant.

Restaurant A is ____expensive____.

Restaurant B is _____than Restaurant A.

Restaurant C is _____most_____restaurant.

**B**   Complete the chart with the missing words. Then check your answers with a partner.

| The superlative form of adjectives | | | | | |
|---|---|---|---|---|---|
| **One syllable** | | **Two syllables** | | **Three or more syllables** | |
| _____ | the sweetest | simple | _____ | _____ | the most expensive |
| large | _____ | _____ | the spiciest | delicious | _____ |
| big | the biggest | _____ | the most crowded | interesting | _____ |

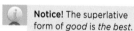

**Notice!** The superlative form of *good* is *the best*.

**C**   Complete the restaurant profile with the superlative form of the adjectives in parentheses. Then answer these questions:

1. Why is this restaurant unusual? Why do people like it?

2. Does it sound interesting to you? Why or why not?

Are you looking for an interesting place to have a meal? One of (1) _____ (unusual) places in the world is Beijing's Dark Restaurant— where you eat in a completely dark room! Dark Restaurant is one of (2) _____(trendy) spots* in China. For many, it is also (3) _____ (popular) place to go on a first date. "It's (4) _____(good) way to get to know someone," says Zhi-ying Chen, a visitor to the restaurant. "In the dark, you can relax and talk." Chen adds, "I also had one of (5) _____(delicious) meals of my life." His girlfriend agrees. "It was (6) _____(weird) but (7) _____(interesting) eating experience I ever had!"

*spot = place

**D**   Work with a partner. Use these adjectives to talk about restauarants you know.

| | | |
|---|---|---|
| noisy | trendy | cheap |
| boring | romantic | bad |

*Bob's Bistro is the noisiest restaurant I know.*

# 5 Writing    Restaurant review

**A**    You are a restaurant reviewer for a popular website. Choose a restaurant you know and make some notes. Then write a review.

Amazon Sun [★★★★★]

Amazon Sun is the best Brazilian restaurant in town. The food is delicious, the staff is friendly, and the prices are moderate. One of the tastiest dishes on the menu is the feijoada completa — a traditional dish of meat, beans, and Brazilian spices. It's excellent!

Amazon Sun is also one of the trendiest places to go these days, so be sure to make a reservation. Enjoy!

Restaurant: Amazon Sun

Food: Brazilian

Prices: Moderate

Location: Downtown

Service: Friendly

**B**    Read your partner's review. Do you want to try the restaurant? Why?

# 6 Communication    Comparing foods

**A**    Complete this chart with foods you know.

| Spicy foods | Sweet foods | Expensive foods | Traditional foods |
| --- | --- | --- | --- |
| | | | |
| | | | |
| | | | |
| | | | |

**B**    Compare your list with a partner's. Tell your partner which food you think is . . .

> I think tiramisu is the most delicious food on the list.

the most delicious      the most expensive      the hardest to prepare at home

the cheapest to buy      the healthiest      the worst for you

**C**    With your partner, create a menu for a new restaurant using many of the foods your group's members have written. Divide the menu into sections (appetizers, entrées, drinks, desserts). Include prices.

**D**    Post your menus for the class to see. Who has the best menu? Why?

 Check out the World Link video.    Practice your English online at http://elt.heinle.com/worldlink

## 1   Vocabulary Link   What are the chances?

**A**   Look at the pictures and the title of the article below. What do you think it's about? Tell your partner.

**B**   Now read the article. Then put the events of the story in order from 1-8.

____ Carmen read the letter.
____ The couple parted.
__1_ Carmen went to England.
____ Steve and Carmen got together again.

____ Carmen met Steve. They fell in love.
____ Years later, workmen found the letter.
____ Carmen's mother got the letter but then she lost it.
____ Steve wrote a letter to Carmen.

## Letter reunites* lovers

In the mid 1990s, Carmen Ruiz Perez and Steve Smith met and fell in love. Carmen, from Spain, was studying in Steve's hometown of Devon, England. They dated for a year, but then Carmen got a job in Paris and the couple had to separate.

After Carmen left, Steve realized he still loved her. Did she love him? He took a chance and wrote a letter to Carmen's address in Paris. Unfortunately, she no longer lived there. Luckily, Steve had Carmen's home address in Spain. He sent a letter to her mother's house. Her mother got the letter, but it fell behind a piece of furniture in her house and was lost. Steve never heard from Carmen.

Several years later, workmen were fixing her mother's house and they found the letter by accident**. What good luck! Carmen read the note and contacted Steve. The couple met and soon married. Steve says he's lucky to have Carmen. "I missed my chance with her the first time. But in the end, everything worked out for the best."

* reunite: to bring two or more things together again

** by accident: by chance, without planning

**C**   Find a word or phrase in blue in the article that has the opposite meaning of each word or phrase in the chart. Compare answers with a partner.

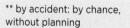

| word or phrase | opposite |
|---|---|
| reunite | |
| unfortunately | |
| on purpose | by accident |
| bad luck | |
| unlucky | |
| didn't try something difficult or risky | took a chance |
| ended badly | |
| had an opportunity to do something | missed a chance |

**ASK ANSWER**
Retell Steve and Carmen's story in your own words. Why was this couple lucky?

## 2 Listening  Lucky you!

**A** Discuss the questions with a partner.

1. Do you think you're a lucky person? Why or why not?

2. Do you ever do things for good luck? For example, do you wear a certain color or say special words?

CD 1
Track 14

**B** You are going to hear a man give a talk. Listen and choose the best title for it.

a. Good Things Happen . . . by Accident!

b. Why Are Some People Luckier Than Others?

c. Better Luck Next Time!

d. Beliefs About Luck Around the World

CD 1
Track 15

**C** Listen. Circle the correct answer.

1. Lucky / Unlucky people are very careful.

2. Lucky / Unlucky people take chances.

3. Lucky / Unlucky people listen to their feelings.

4. Lucky / Unlucky people focus on the facts.

5. Lucky / Unlucky people expect bad things to happen.

6. Lucky / Unlucky people expect good things to happen.

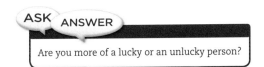

ASK ANSWER

Are you more of a lucky or an unlucky person?

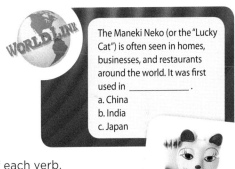

The Maneki Neko (or the "Lucky Cat") is often seen in homes, businesses, and restaurants around the world. It was first used in _____ .
a. China
b. India
c. Japan

## 3 Pronunciation  **Past tense vowel shifts**

**A** Complete the sentences below with the past tense form of each verb.

1. I _____ (hear) an interesting story on the radio last night.

2. Steve and Carmen _____ (meet) in England.

3. Later, she _____ (take) a job in Paris and they separated.

4. Steve _____ (know) he still loved Carmen so he _____ (write) a letter to her.

5. Carmen's mother _____ (get) the letter, but then she _____ (lose) it.

6. Later, workmen _____ (find) the letter and Carmen _____ (read) it. What luck!

7. I _____ (think) this was a good story.

**B** With a partner, say both the present and past tense of each verb in **A**. What do you notice about the vowels in these verbs?

CD 1
Track 16

**C** Listen to the sentences in **A**. How was your pronunciation of the verbs?

**D** Practice saying the sentences with a partner.

## 4 Speaking    I bet she's good at math.

**CD 1
Track 17**

**A** Nico and Sandra are talking about a news article. Listen and answer the questions.

1. What did a woman in New York City do?

2. How did she do it?

3. What is she going to do now?

**Sandra:** Anything interesting in today's news?

**Nico:** Yeah, I'm reading about a woman in New York City. She just won $25,000.

**Sandra:** That's a lot of money. Did she win the lottery?

**Nico:** No, she guessed the correct number of candies in a jar.

**Sandra:** Really? How many were there?

**Nico:** 7,954.

**Sandra:** Wow. That was a lucky guess!

**Nico:** Oh, I doubt she guessed. I bet she's good at math. The article says she won a similar contest in the past.

**Sandra:** So, what's she going to do with the money?

**Nico:** I don't know. She'll probably go on vacation or use it for school.

**B** Practice the conversation with a partner.

## 5 Speaking Strategy

**A** On the lines below, write two things about yourself that are true. Write one thing that is a lie.

_____

_____

_____

**B** Get into a group of 3-4 people and do the following:

1. One person tells the group his or her sentences.

2. The others . . .

   • ask the speaker questions to find out which sentence is a lie.
   • use the Useful Expressions to discuss their ideas.
   • guess which sentence is a lie. If you guess correctly, you get a point.

3. Change roles and repeat steps 1 and 2.

| Useful Expressions: Talking about possibility | |
|---|---|
| **Saying something is likely** | |
| I bet (that) | Marco plays drums in a band. |
| Marco **probably** | plays drums in a band. |
| **Maybe / Perhaps** | Marco plays drums in a band. |
| **To disagree that it is likely** | |
| I doubt (that) | Marco plays drums in a band. |

*I bet Marco plays drums in a band. He owns a pair of drum sticks.*

*Well, maybe he plays drums, but not in a band.*

*Yeah, I doubt he plays drums in a band. I bet that's the lie.*

## 6 Language Link    Stative verbs

**A** Look at the chart of stative verbs below. Then add the verbs in the box to the chart.

> hate    hear    like    own    smell    understand

| Stative Verbs | | | | |
|---|---|---|---|---|
| Thinking verbs | Having verbs | Feeling verbs | Sensing verbs | Other verbs |
| believe | belong | appreciate | _____ | seem |
| know | have | _____ | see | look |
| think | _____ | _____ | _____ | mean |
| _____ | | love | taste | cost |
| | | | | need |

**B** These sentences use stative verbs. The sentences in Column A are correct. The ones in Column B are incorrect. What can you say about stative verbs? Tell a partner.

| Column A (correct) | Column B (incorrect) |
|---|---|
| I own more than 100 books. | ~~I am owning more than 100 books.~~ |
| We know many words in English. | ~~We are knowing many words in English.~~ |
| He seems like a nice person. | ~~He is seeming like a nice person.~~ |

**C** Read the paragraphs below. If an underlined verb is used incorrectly, circle it and correct it. Then take turns reading the paragraphs aloud with a partner.

Winning the lottery—to most people, it <u>seems</u> like great luck. Unfortunately, for the winners, it's often the opposite. Ian Walters, for example, won a million pounds in a lottery in the UK five years ago. "When you <u>win</u> the lottery, suddenly you <u>are having</u> a lot of money," he explains. "You <u>are thinking</u> it will last forever, and you <u>spend</u> it quickly." And then one day, the money is gone. "Two years ago, I had a big house," Ian says. "These days, <u>I'm living</u> with my sister and <u>I'm working</u> in a small cafe. Luckily, I still <u>am owning</u> my car." So, what's Ian's advice? "In the past, I <u>believed</u> money could buy happiness," he says. "Now I <u>am knowing</u> this isn't true."

## 7 Communication    **Strange but true stories**

**A**  Work with a partner. Choose one story—Story A or Story B—below. Cover the other story up—do <u>not</u> read it. Read the story you chose. Think about answers to these questions as you read:

1. Who is the story about?

2. What happened?

### Story A

David Brown and Michelle Kitson met in an unusual way. One night, David went out with his friends. The next morning, he woke up, thinking of a phone number. He didn't know whose it was, so he texted the person. "Did I meet you last night?" he asked in his message. In another town, Michelle got David's text. She didn't know him. She answered, "No. Who are you and where are you from?" David answered and the two continued texting. Finally, David took a chance and asked to meet Michelle. She agreed and now they are dating. David still can't believe his good luck. Why did he dream about Michelle's phone number? He still can't explain it.

### Story B

On the morning of February 19, Corina Sanchez said goodbye to her husband and 17-year-old son and went to work. "It was a typical day," Corina remembers. "But then at lunchtime, I started to feel strange—really nervous—but I didn't know why. Two hours later, I got a phone call from my son—he was in a car accident!" Luckily, Corina's son wasn't hurt, but how did she know something was wrong? She still can't explain it.

**B**  Work again with your partner and do the following:

**Student A:** In your own words, tell your story to your partner.
**Student B:** Listen to your partner's story. Take notes to answer the questions. Then switch roles.

1. Who is the story about? _____

2. What happened? _____

_____

**C**  Can you explain what happened to David and Corina? Discuss your ideas with your partner. Then compare your ideas with another pair. Which explanation is the best?

> How did David know Michelle's phone number?

> Well, I bet he ...

# Unsolved Mysteries

## Lesson B   Mysteries of the world

> "I first heard 'The Hum' in the 1970s. Only some people can hear it. There are lots of possible explanations: electrical wires, traffic noise, cell phone towers … I don't know what to think." —Jaqui Moore, Australia

## 1   Vocabulary Link   An unsolved mystery

**A**   Read the information below. What is "The Hum"? Who hears it? What causes it?

> "I hear a low humming sound all the time. It sounds like a car engine. It's very mysterious. I hope someone solves this mystery soon because it's driving me crazy!" —Alan Black, England

> "No one can figure out the source of the humming sound. We have a lot of theories, but no answers yet."—Dr. Harini Gupta, scientist, India

> "We're investigating 'The Hum'. I can't even prove it exists because I can't hear a thing. But many people say that they hear it. It just doesn't make sense." —Brian Lam, police officer, U.S.

**B**   Match words 1–8 to their definitions (a–f). Some definitions match more than one word.

a. a guess or idea

b. to show that something is definitely true

c. to find an answer to a question or problem

d. to study something closely to find the truth

e. to be logical or understandable

f. strange or unusual

_____ 1. mysterious

_____ 2. figure out

_____ 3. make sense

_____ 4. explanation

_____ 5. investigate

_____ 6. theory

_____ 7. prove

_____ 8. solve

**C**   Write the noun or verb form of these words. Then compare your answers with your partner.

**ASK  ANSWER**

Look again at the theories in **A**. Can you think of other explanations for "The Hum"? In your opinion, which explanation makes the most sense?

| Noun | Verb |
|---|---|
| _____ | explain |
| investigation | _____ |
| solution | _____ |
| proof | _____ |

## 2 Listening    Full moon fever

**A** Look at the chart. What do you think it's showing us? Tell a partner.

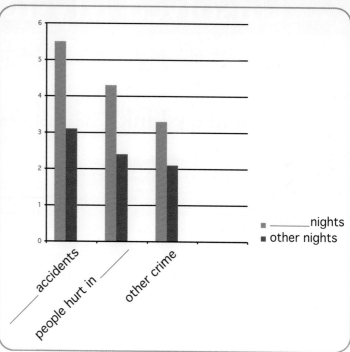

■ _____nights
■ other nights

accidents
people hurt in _____
other crime

CD 1
Track 18

**B** You are going to hear a news report. Do the following:

1. Listen and complete the chart in **A**.

2. What are officials planning to do? Write your idea and then tell a partner.

   _____

CD 1
Track 19

**C** Look at your answer to question 2 in **B**. Why are officials planning to do this? Listen to the rest of the report. Complete the sentences below.

1. The city needs more _____.

2. _____ nights are
   _____ than other nights.

3. More people _____.

> **ASK ANSWER**
>
> What are London officials planning to do? Why? Use your answers in **B** and **C** to explain.
>
> What are some beliefs about the moon in your country?

## 3 Reading    Mysterious artwork

**A** Look at the title and photos on page 29 and answer the questions below. Then read the interview once to check your answers.

1. What do you think the things in the photos are?

2. Who do you think made them?

**B** Read the passage again. Then write the questions below in the correct places in the interview. Two questions are extra.

- What was the purpose of the lines?
- How do the local people feel about the lines?
- What exactly are the Nazca Lines?
- Who created these unusual ground drawings?
- How did they do it—especially without modern technology?
- Can anyone visit the Nazca Lines?

# MYSTERIOUS ARTWORK

**Interviewer:** The Nazca Desert in Peru is home to one of the most unusual sites in the world. In this issue, we talk with Dr. Gabriel Reyes about the Nazca Lines and why they are one of history's greatest mysteries.

So, Dr. Reyes, tell us: _____

**Dr. Reyes:** On the ground for almost 60 kilometers (37 miles) in the Peruvian desert are hundreds of line drawings of different animals, humans, insects, and other symbols. These drawings, known as the Nazca Lines, are very large. Some are over 200 meters (600 feet) long and can only be seen correctly from the sky.

**Interviewer:** _____

**Dr. Reyes:** For years, people had different theories. Some thought visitors from another planet drew them—maybe because the lines are best seen from a plane. Today, though, scientists believe the Nazca people created the images. They lived in the area from 200 B.C. to the 7th century A.D. and probably made the drawings over 1,500 years ago.

**Interviewer:** 1,500 years ago? _____

**Dr. Reyes:** Most likely they used simple tools. A team probably planned what they wanted a certain image to look like. Then they worked together and made the drawings in the desert ground. They didn't need planes or other modern equipment.

**Interviewer:** _____

**Dr. Reyes:** Good question. We still can't figure out why the Nazca people drew these large pictures on the ground - images you can really only see from the sky. Many scientists think the images might be religious symbols. Others believe the lines may be a large map; perhaps the Nazca people used the lines to find water in the desert. Still others think the lines were a special type of calendar. As I say, scientists are still investigating.

**C** The statements below are wrong. Change them so they are correct. Underline the sentence(s) in the interview that helped you make your changes.

1. North Americans probably created the lines in the year 1500 A. D.

2. The lines are small and must be looked at closely on the ground.

3. It was probably difficult for people to make the lines without modern tools.

4. Scientists now know what the Nazca Lines were used for—a calendar.

**D** Look back at the four questions in the interview. Take turns asking and answering these with a partner. When you answer a question, use your own words. Try not to look back at the reading.

# 4 Language Link  Modals of present possibility

**A** Look at the picture and read the question and the answers in the chart. Then complete sentences 1 and 2 below with the correct modals.

1. Use _____ to say something is possible.

2. Use _____ to say something is not possible.

**B** Read the note about short answers. Then complete the dialogs below. Practice them with a partner.

| Who's that man with Marta? | | |
|---|---|---|
| Subject | Modal | Main Verb |
| He | **may** **might** **could** | be | her dad. They look alike. |
| | **can't** **couldn't** | be | her brother. He's much older than Marta. |

1. A: Is Luis from Brazil?
   B: He _____. He visits Sao Paulo all the time.

2. A: How old is Alice?
   B: I don't know. She _____ 30 or 35.
   C: She _____. She graduated from college in 1980.

3. A: Do you think "The Hum" is real?
   B: It _____. A lot of people hear it.

4. A: Where's Jane?
   B: I'm not sure. She _____ with Myra. They always hang out together.
   A: She _____. Myra is on vacation.

5. A: Are Yuko's parents in Japan now?
   B: They _____ there. I just saw them yesterday.

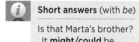
**Short answers** (with *be*)
Is that Marta's brother?
It **might/could** <u>be</u>.
It **can't/couldn't** <u>be</u>.

**C** Read each situation. Think of two possible explanations for each one.

1. Your friend isn't answering her cell phone.

2. You received a mysterious package in the mail.

3. The teacher isn't here today.

4. A new student in our class is quiet.

# 5 Writing  A strange event

**A** Read the paragraph on the right. Then write one or two more paragraphs to finish the story.

**B** Exchange your story with a partner. As you read your partner's story, answer the questions. Then tell your partner your answers.

1. What was the sound Danny heard?

2. What is a good title for your partner's story?

Danny woke up. "What was that noise?" he wondered. It was dark and Danny couldn't see. He turned on the light and looked at the clock. It was 2:00 a.m. Bang! There was the noise again. "What could it be?" Danny thought nervously. His parents weren't at home and his sister was at a friend's house. Danny opened his bedroom door and walked out to investigate. ...

# 6  Communication    **What's your theory?**

**A**   Look at the photos and read the notes about these unsolved mysteries.
Then answer the question below about each.

The Chupacabra

The Yonaguni Monument

The Marfa Lights

**What:** It's a creature about 1.2 meters (4 feet) tall with red eyes and big teeth. It can jump high. It kills animals and drinks their blood. It's seen only at night.

**Where:** All over North and South America and parts of Russia

**When:** Was first seen in 1995

**What do you think each thing is?**

a. a large dog or other animal
b. a man in a costume
c. a terrible monster
d. your idea: _____

**What:** It's a large underwater rock formation—about 25 meters (82 feet) high. It looks like pyramids seen in Egypt and the Americas.

**Where:** In the Pacific Ocean, near Japan

**When:** Was discovered in 1986

a. an underwater city
b. an old Japanese pyramid
c. nothing, just some rocks
d. your idea: _____

**What:** They're lights that appear suddenly in the night sky. Often, there are two or three of them. They are about the size of a basketball. Sometimes they fly close to people's houses.

**Where:** In the desert near the town of Marfa, Texas (U.S.)

**When:** Were first seen in 1883

a. lights from a car or plane
b. some kind of strange weather
c. space aliens
d. your idea: _____

   **B**   Work in a group of 3 or 4 people. Discuss your answers to the question in **A**.
Which is the most likely explanation?

> The Marfa Lights might be lights from a car or plane...

> No, they can't be because...

   **C**   Can you think of other unsolved mysteries like the ones in **A**?
What do you think they are? Tell your group about them.

 Check out the World Link video.     Practice your English online at http://elt.heinle.com/worldlink

# Review: Units 1-3

## 1  Storyboard

**A**  Susan, Maya, and Bruno work together. Look at the pictures and complete the conversations. For some blanks, more than one answer is possible.

**B**  Practice the conversation with two people. Then change roles and practice again.

**C**  Introduce a friend to another friend. Invite both friends out to dinner.

# 2 See It and Say It

**A** Below is a page from Anna Lopez's high school yearbook. She graduated in 1998. Read what her classmates wrote in her yearbook. How did Anna know each person? Discuss your ideas with a partner.

*Sorry I didn't get to know you better, Anna. Good luck in college! Bobby*

*Hey, Anna! Best friends 4-ever! Rachel*

**Michael Evans**    **Bobby Leong**    **Anna Lopez**    **Rachel Williams**

*We're graduating, but you'll always be my girl, Anna. ~Michael*

**B** Look at the people in **A** as they are today.

1. What are their relationships now?

2. Choose one of the pictures below. Make up a story about it. Answer these questions:
   • What happened to the people in your picture after high school?
   • How did they meet again?

3. Tell your partner the story of your picture.

Bobby and Anna

Rachel and Michael

# 3 Listening

**A** Look at the photos below. What words would you use to describe these things? Tell your partner.

CD 1
Track 20

**B** Four people are going to talk about their eating habits. Listen. Which food does each person like or eat a lot? Match a speaker (1, 2, 3, or 4) with the correct photo(s).

CD 1
Track 21

**C** Read sentences 1–3 below. Then listen. Choose the correct answer for each sentence.

1. If you *get in shape*, you . . .

   a. gain weight.

   b. do things to be healthier.

   c. don't do much exercise.

2. If food tastes *bland*, it has . . .

   a. a strong taste.

   b. a lot of spices in it.

   c. no flavor.

3. If you *have a sweet tooth*, you . . .

   a. like sugary foods.

   b. can't eat sweets.

   c. are a good cook.

**D** Work with a partner and do the following:

   1. Write three more food or drink items in the chart below.

| food or drink item | Speaker 1 | Speaker 2 | Speaker 3 | Speaker 4 |
|---|---|---|---|---|
| 1. pizza | | | | |
| 2. a glass of milk | | | | |
| 3. _____ | | | | |
| 4. _____ | | | | |
| 5. _____ | | | | |

CD 1
Track 20

   2. Listen again. Which speaker (1, 2, 3, or 4) probably eats the items on your list often? Check (✓) the correct person.

   3. Discuss your answers with a partner. Talk about the possibilities.

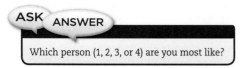

ASK ANSWER

Which person (1, 2, 3, or 4) are you most like?

I doubt that Speaker 1 eats pizza because...

# 4 Wonders of the World

Use the adjectives in the box to ask and answer questions about these monuments with a partner.

| | | | |
|---|---|---|---|
| beautiful | interesting | popular | strange |
| impressive | old | remote | tall |

The Great Wall of China

The Eiffel Tower

Roman Colosseum

The statues on Easter Island

Which monument is the oldest?

Well, the statues on Easter Island look old, but I bet the Roman Colosseum is older.

# 5 I'm Reading an Interesting Book.

**A** Choose three words from the box. Write three sentences about yourself in your notebook. Use the simple present or the present continuous.

| | | | |
|---|---|---|---|
| eat | know | like | study |
| read | own | work | |

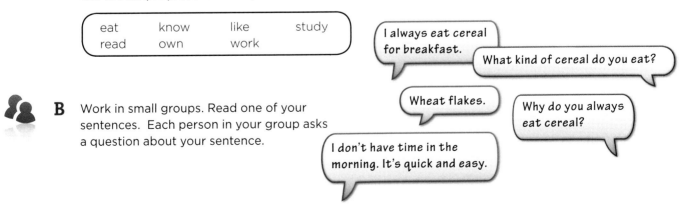

I always eat cereal for breakfast.

What kind of cereal do you eat?

**B** Work in small groups. Read one of your sentences. Each person in your group asks a question about your sentence.

Wheat flakes.

Why do you always eat cereal?

I don't have time in the morning. It's quick and easy.

# 4 Today's Trends

## Lesson A  Family trends

## 1  Vocabulary Link  Family trends

**A**  Complete the sentences below with a word or phrase from the box. Compare your answers with a partner.

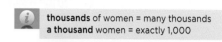

**thousands** of women = many thousands
**a thousand** women = exactly 1,000

**trend** = a change or development toward something different

> half    percent    thousands

### American Family Trends

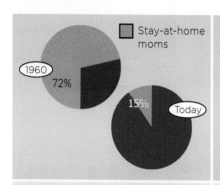

Stay-at-home moms
1960
72%
15%
Today

Divorce rate
50%
1966    Today

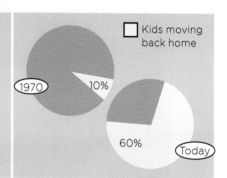

Kids moving back home
1970
10%
60%
Today

In 1960, over 70 percent of homes had a working father and stay-at-home mother. Today, this number has dropped to 15 percent because _____ of women now have jobs outside the home.

The number of divorces today is almost twice as high as in 1966. In the 1960s, a quarter (25%) of all marriages ended in divorce. Today, nearly _____ (50%) of all marriages end in divorce.

The average American leaves home between the ages of 18 and 20. In 1970, 10% of these people moved back with their parents after leaving home. Today, that number has risen to sixty _____.

**B**  Find a blue word or phrase in **A** that has a similar meaning to each word or phrase below.

1. almost _____

2. more than _____

3. two times as high as _____

4. usual, typical _____

5. fifty percent _____

6. increased _____

7. decreased _____

8. twenty-five percent, one-fourth _____

**C**  Complete the sentences with a blue word in **A**. Which words are used to talk about an exact number or amount? Which talk about an approximate (not exact) amount?

1. Mary's birthday is next month. She's _____ 12 years old.

2. _____ of 40 is 20.

3. There were _____ of people at the concert—maybe 20,000 or more.

4. Bob is _____ 30. Maybe he's 34 or 35.

5. Class A has 15 people and B has 30. Class B is _____ as big as Class A.

ASK  ANSWER

In your opinion, which trends in **A** are positive? Which are negative? Why?

Are these trends similar or different in your country? Explain.

## 2 Listening   Still at home

CD 1
Track 22

**A**  You will hear three people talking. Listen and answer the question.

What trend are the people talking about?

    a. people getting married later

    b. children living with their parents longer

    c. people having fewer children

CD 1
Track 22

**B**  Look at your answer in **A** and read the questions below.
Then listen again and answer the questions.

  1. In each place, what is causing this trend? Match the places with the reasons from the box.

    Italy    _____

    Japan    _____

    the UK    _____

> a. Housing costs are high.    c. Getting a job is difficult.
>
> b. Education is expensive.    d. People are waiting to get married.

  2. Which person does NOT think the trend is good?

    a. Alessandro       b. Aya       c. Evan

CD 1
Track 22

**C**  Listen again and connect the information in the three columns.

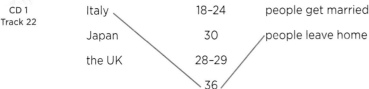

Italy      18–24      people get married

Japan      30      people leave home

the UK      28–29

           36

> In Italy, the average age that
> people leave home is 36. People
> wait to move out because ...

**D**  Tell a partner about the trends in Italy, Japan, and the UK.
Use your answers in **B** and **C** to help you.

## 3 Pronunciation   Unstressed *of* in rapid speech

CD 1
Track 23

**A**  Listen. Notice the pronunciation of the word *of*.

  1. Most of my friends still live with their parents.

  2. A lot of people are getting married later.

  3. Leaving your parents' house is part of becoming an adult.

 **Note:** In rapid speech, the final *f* sound in *of* is usually dropped before a consonant sound.

CD 1
Track 24

**B**  Listen and complete the sentences. Then practice saying them aloud.

  1. _____ the kids in my family still live at home.

  2. _____ my friends are studying in New York City.

  3. _____ people get divorced every year.

  4. _____ them have children.

## 4 Speaking   **I know what you're saying, but . . .**

CD 1
Track 25

**A** Listen to the conversation. Then answer the questions with a partner.

1. Carla and her dad are fighting about something. What?

2. Who do you agree with—Carla or her dad?

| | |
|---|---|
| Carla: | Dad, can I talk to you for a minute? |
| Dad: | Sure, what's up? |
| Carla: | Well, my friend Marta is going to see a concert tomorrow night and she invited me to go. |
| Dad: | Tomorrow night? But tomorrow's Tuesday. Sorry, Carla, but no. |
| Carla: | Dad! You *never* let me do anything. |
| Dad: | That's not true, Carla. You do lots of things. But the concert ends late and you have school on Wednesday. |
| Carla: | I know what you're saying, Dad, but it's just one night. And all of my friends are going. |
| Dad: | Sorry, Carla, but the answer is still "no." |
| Carla: | Oh, Dad, you're so unfair! |

**B** Practice the conversation with a partner.

## 5 Speaking Strategy

| Useful Expressions: Disagreeing | |
|---|---|
| **Politely** | **Strongly** |
| I know what you're saying, but . . . | That's not true. |
| Sorry, but I disagree. / I don't agree. | I totally / completely disagree. |
| I hear you, but . . . [very informal] | Oh, come on! / Are you serious? [very informal] |

**A** Work with a partner. One person is the parent. The other person is the son or daughter.

1. Choose a situation from the box. Think of reasons for and against it.

2. Create a new conversation similar to the one above. In your dialog, use at least two Useful Expressions.

**B** Get together with another pair.

- **Pair 1:** Perform your dialog for another pair.

- **Pair 2:** Listen. Who do you agree with—the parent or child? Why?

**C** Switch roles and do **B** again.

> **Parents: Your son or daughter wants to . . .**
> - go on a date
> - visit another country by himself or herself
> - get a part-time job
> - your own idea: _____

## 6 Language Link   Quantity expressions

100% all (of)
most (of)
a lot (of)
some (of)
a couple (of)
0% none (of)

**A**   Read the information about six families from around the world.
Then write *all*, *most*, *a lot*, *some*, *a couple*, or *none* in the blanks below.

ⓘ a couple = two

|  | the SHAW family | the IKEDA family | the OLIVEIRA family | the CHOI family | the DEMIR family | the KUMAR family |
|---|---|---|---|---|---|---|
| hometown | Chicago | Tokyo | Sao Paulo | Seoul | Istanbul | New Delhi |
| language | English | Japanese | Portuguese | Korean | Turkish | English |
| housing | house | apartment | apartment | apartment | apartment | apartment |
| transportation | car | subway | bus | car | car | bus |
| wife works | restaurant | office | hotel | office | office | office |
| children | no | yes | yes | yes | yes | yes |

1. _____ of the families live in big cities.

2. _____ of the families speak English.

3. _____ of them speak French.

4. _____ of the families live in apartments.

5. _____ of them own cars.

6. _____ of the families have a working wife.

7. _____ of the wives work in an office.

8. _____ of the families have children.

**B**   Complete the sentences below with the correct word(s).

1. Most / Most of people want to be happy.

2. Most / Most of my friends speak English, but none / none of them speak it at home.

3. Some / Some of students live with their families because it's cheaper.

4. Most / Most of our neighbors have children; a couple / a couple of them have pets, too.

5. All / All of parents want their children to do well in school.

6. Some / Some of the teachers at my school are really strict.

ⓘ **Using *of***

(students everywhere) **Most students** work hard.

(specific students) **Most of the students** <u>in my class</u> work hard.

Not: ~~Most of students in my class work hard.~~

**C**   Tell your partner about the families you know using *all (of)*, *most (of)*, *a lot (of)*, *some (of)*, *a couple (of)*, or *none (of)*. Use the list below.

have children                    speak English

have a stay-at-home wife          own more than one car

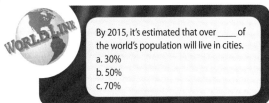

By 2015, it's estimated that over ____ of the world's population will live in cities.
a. 30%
b. 50%
c. 70%

## 7 Communication    **What should they do?**

**A**    Read each situation below. For each one, choose the answer you agree with or write your own idea.

Luis has an older brother and sister. They both go to City University and Luis's father wants him to go there, too. Luis doesn't want to, but if he doesn't go to City, his father will not pay for his school. What should Luis do?

1. Go to City University like his father wants.
2. Start at City University and then later transfer (change) to another school.
3. Get a job, save his money, and pay for his own education.
4. Your idea: _____

Yukiko's sixteen-year-old brother is hanging out with some bad people. He isn't going to class and he is fighting at school. Yukiko is worried about her brother. What should she do?

1. Wait a little longer. Maybe things will change.
2. Talk to her brother. Tell him her feelings.
3. Tell her parents about her brother.
4. Your idea: _____

Josh is dating a girl named Holly. Josh loves Holly, but Josh's parents don't like her. This weekend is Josh's birthday. His parents are having a big party and they have invited all of his friends—except Holly. What should Josh do?

1. Talk to his parents and tell them to invite Holly.
2. Just bring Holly to the party.
3. Skip the party and spend the day with Holly.
4. Your idea: _____

**B**    Get into a group of four or five people. Talk about your opinions in **A** with your group. Explain the reasons for your choice.

> I think Luis should go to City University.

> Yeah, I agree . . .

> Sorry, but I totally disagree with both of you. I think . . .

**C**    Look back at each situation in **A**. How many people in your group agreed with answers 1, 2, or 3? How many came up with their own answers? Compare your results with another group.

> Most of the people in our group think Luis should go to City University.

> Only one person in our group thinks Luis should go to City University. Most of us think . . .

# Today's Trends

## 1  Vocabulary Link  Fashion trends

**A**  Read about some of these decades' popular fashions. Then, with a partner, use the words in blue to describe each photo on the time line.

 in = popular, fashionable
a look = a style

# What was in?

**The 80s**

Conservative business suits with big shoulders for both men and women

Casual but sporty clothes known as the "preppy" look

Bright colors and big jewelry

Dramatic makeup and hairstyles and the color black—especially with punks and goths

**The 90s**

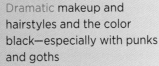

Grunge: a casual—almost sloppy—look of ripped jeans and old shirts

Hip-hop fashion: baseball caps, oversized shirts, and baggy pants

**The 00s**

skinny (fitted) jeans

Pointy shoes and boots for both men and women

Body piercings

Retro 80s fashion (dramatic hairstyles, bright colors)

**B**  Discuss the questions with a partner.

1. What styles are "in" today? Describe each look.

2. Which words describe your look? What clothes do you usually wear?

> **Describing your look**
>
> casual / comfortable, colorful, conservative, dramatic, fun, retro, sloppy, sporty, stylish, unique

## 2 Listening    You've got the look.

**A**   With a partner, describe the people's clothes in the photos below.

**B**   Listen to a makeover TV show. Number the people (1, 2, or 3) that the speakers talk about. One picture is extra.

 If you **get a makeover**, you do things to make yourself more attractive.

CD 1
Track 26

CD 1
Track 27

**C**   Look at your answers (1, 2, and 3) in **B**. Then do the following:

1. What style problem does each person have?
   Can you guess what the solutions are?

2. Listen to the rest of the show and complete the chart below.
   Use only one word per blank.

ASK  ANSWER

Do you agree with the hosts' suggestions? Why or why not?

| Style Problem | Style solution |
|---|---|
| Brad's look is too conservative / sloppy. | He could wear a _____ new _____. |
| Tamara's clothes are too baggy / sporty. | She should wear something more _____ like a pair of _____ jeans and a fun _____. |
| Mimi's look is too casual / mismatched. | She should choose a single _____ and one or two _____ that _____. |

## 3 Reading    Trendspotting

**A**   Read the job advertisement. What do you think a *trendspotter* does? Who would hire a trendspotter?

Are you between the ages of 15 and 22? Do you like fashion and music? Do you know what's hot? You could be a **trendspotter!**

- Try new products!
- Participate in surveys!
- Receive free samples!
Call now: 555-2200.

**B**  Brooke is 18 years old. She works as a trendspotter. What does she do? Read her blog postings and check your answers in **A**.

---

Home  About  Archives  Mail  RSS

March **17**  **Part-time Job**

💬 0 Comments | Posted by Brooke

Today I started my new part-time job as a trendspotter. I was nervous and didn't know what to expect. Well, guess what! It was a lot of fun! I'm telling all my friends, "You should think about becoming a trendspotter, too!"

This morning, we had to report to a recording studio by 10 a.m. The "Trends Coordinator," Mandy, explained the schedule. _____. That was really cool!

Next we sat around a big table in a room. _____. Mandy gave each person three cards. One card said "Yes—All the way!" Another said, "It's OK." The third one said, "No way!" We listened to about 10 different songs. After each song, we had to hold up a card. They played some hip-hop, rock, heavy metal, and dance music. The heavy metal was "No way" for me!

March **24**  **Gifted**

💬 0 Comments | Posted by Brooke

Do you know the rock group called "Gifted"? They're really popular right now. _____. Too bad we missed them. Anyway, they have a new CD coming out on Jtunz soon. We saw six different CD covers. (I guess they are trying to choose one.) This time, we didn't have any cards. Instead, we just talked about the covers we liked. Mandy asked us questions: "Which ones do you like?"  "Why do you like them?"  "Would you buy a CD with this cover?"

We finished at 12:30. We meet again next week at a boutique downtown. We will look at some new fashions. Each week we go to a different location. Oh, and we also received a music gift card for our work. This "job" doesn't pay, but we get free stuff!

That's all for now!

---

**C**  Check (✓) the sentence(s) Brooke would say about being a trendspotter. Compare your answers with a partner.

____ It's kind of boring.

____ You can make good money.

____ You get free things.

____ You work with famous people.

____ People ask your opinion about lots of things.

____ You work once a week at different places.

**D**  Below are extra sentences from the reading.
Add each one to the correct place in the reading.
One sentence is extra.

Yesterday, they were here in the studio.

I can't wait for our next meeting!

Then she gave us a tour of the studio.

There were about ten of us.

> **ASK  ANSWER**
>
> Why do you think companies use trendspotters?
> Do you think it's a good idea?
>
> Would you like to be a trendspotter? Why or why not?

# 4 Language Link   Giving advice with *could, should, ought to,* and *had better*

**A**   Read the question about cell phones and the three answers.
Then complete the sentences with the modal verbs in blue.

Q: I want to buy a new cell phone. What should I do?

A1: You could ask your friends or a salesperson for their suggestions.

A2: You should read *Consumer Advice* magazine. They rate the different phones.

A3: You'd better be careful. Some of the best cell phones are really expensive.

 you'd better = you had better

> In A1, _____ is used to make a suggestion (about two or more things).
>
> In A2, _____ is used to give advice. Ought to can also be used to give advice.
>
> In A3, _____ is used to give stronger advice. It can sound like a warning.

**B**   Complete the conversations with the expressions in the boxes.
Use each expression only once.

> shouldn't    could    ought to

**Negative forms**

You shouldn't wear a T-shirt to a job interview. It's too casual.

We'd better not drive to the concert. It'll be hard to park.

**Betsy:**   I don't know what to wear to the party tonight.

**Carla:**   You (1) _____ wear your new skinny jeans or black pants.

**Betsy:**   It's a formal dress party.

**Carla:**   Oh, then you (2) _____ wear jeans. They're too casual.
You definitely (3) _____ wear the black pants.

> had better    could    had better not

**Fred:**   I still don't understand this grammar.

**Doug:**   You (4) _____ get some help or you will fail the test. It's on Thursday.

**Fred:**   Maybe I (5) _____ take the test on Friday. That would give me extra time.

**Doug:**   Well, you (6) _____ delay. There's not much time!

**C**   You are going to an informal party. Your partner is going to a formal party. Look at the list and
give advice to each other.

> arrive a little late          wear casual clothes              bring a friend who wasn't invited
>
> bring food for the party      wear a suit or a nice dress      bring flowers or champagne to the host

> You could wear a suit or nice dress.

> You shouldn't wear casual clothes.

## 5 Writing  **What's your advice?**

**A**  Read the post from Sad Sam in Seattle. What is his problem?

**B**  Now write a response to Sam. Give him some advice. Then share your writing with a partner.

## Ask Susie Style

Dear Susie Style,

I need your help! I can't get a job. Everywhere I go, I get the same answer: "No!" My friend says that my appearance is the problem. Here is a picture of me. What do you think? What should I do?

*Sad Sam in Seattle*

## 6 Communication  **Do you need a makeover?**

**A**  Ask your partner the questions. Check (✓) your partner's answers.

| How often do you . . . | often | sometimes | never |
|---|:---:|:---:|:---:|
| 1. wear "the same old thing"? | ☐ | ☐ | ☐ |
| 2. buy something because it's cheap? | ☐ | ☐ | ☐ |
| 3. wear something comfortable but mismatched? | ☐ | ☐ | ☐ |
| 4. wear something until it's completely worn out? | ☐ | ☐ | ☐ |
| 5. leave the house without looking in the mirror? | ☐ | ☐ | ☐ |
| 6. read fashion magazines about new trends? | ☐ | ☐ | ☐ |
| 7. change your hairstyle? | ☐ | ☐ | ☐ |
| 8. go to concerts and listen to new music? | ☐ | ☐ | ☐ |

**B**  Calculate your partner's score. Use the table.

|  | **for questions 1–5** | **or questions 6–8** |
|---|---|---|
| **often** | score 2 points | score 0 points |
| **sometimes** | score 1 point | score 1 point |
| **never** | score 0 points | score 2 points |

**C**  Read the appropriate advice to your partner. What does your partner think of the advice?

| **0–3 points:** You know what's "in" and have a great sense of style. Keep up the great work! | **4–7 points:** You have a good sense of style, but you could change a few things or just try to do something new every week. | **8–12 points:** Your look definitely needs an update. You could change something about your clothing or hairstyle. You should also try to go out more and see what's happening. | **13–16 points:** You scored a lot of points. You'd better think about getting a complete makeover! |
|---|---|---|---|

 Check out the World Link video.    Practice your English online at http://elt.heinle.com/worldlink

## 1  Vocabulary Link  Handy Helpers

**A**  Read the ad below and answer the questions with a partner.

 **an errand:** a short trip you make to do or get something

**a chore:** work you do regularly at home

1. What does Handy Helpers do?

2. Which items on the to-do list are errands?
   Which are chores? Write *E* for *errand* or *C* for *chore* next to each item.

---

### Handy Helpers

Are you a busy person? Do you have too much to do—even on the weekends? Would you like more time to relax? If you answered "yes" to any of these questions, it's time to contact Handy Helpers!

We'll do your chores or run your errands so you can take a break. To learn more about us and the services we offer, call or e-mail us today!

**Click here to make a personal to-do list**

---

**My to-do list**

☐ take the dog for a walk
☐ go grocery shopping
☐ do the dishes
☐ sweep the floors and vacuum the rugs
☐ pick up the dry cleaning
☐ mail a package
☐ do the laundry
☐ take Marty to soccer practice
☐ make dinner

**Other**
☐ make an appointment to get a haircut
☐ make a dinner reservation at restaurant

---

**B**  Complete the sentences below with the correct form of a word or phrase in blue from **A**.

1. All my clothes are dirty. I need to do the _____!

2. Kira's not home. She _____ her younger brothers _____ a movie.

3. My tooth hurts. I need to _____ to see the dentist.

4. The rug in the bedroom is dusty. Can you _____ it?

5. Can you _____ these letters at the post office?

6. I'd like to _____ for six people at 7:00 tonight. Is a table available?

7. Let's _____ the dinner dishes now.

8. Before you _____ any errands, you should _____ a list of the things you need to do.

9. Susan always _____ her children after they finish school.

10. I'm really tired. Let's _____ a _____. We can study again tomorrow.

**C**  Which phrases in **A** use *do*, *make*, or *take*? Complete the chart below.
Can you think of other phrases that start with these words? Add them.

| do | the chores, _____, _____ |
|---|---|
| **make** | dinner, an appointment, _____ |
| **take** | (the dog for) a walk, someone to a place, _____ |

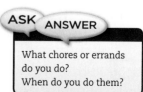

**ASK  ANSWER**

What chores or errands do you do?
When do you do them?

## 2 Listening    I'm calling because . . .

CD 1
Track 28

**A**  You are going to hear four different phone calls. Read the sentences below.
Then listen and circle the correct word(s) to complete each sentence.

1. The woman is calling to make / change a reservation.

2. The man wants to know when he can drop off / pick up his dry cleaning.

3. The man is calling to make / change an appointment.

4. The girl wants her friend to take her to school / the doctor's office.

> ⓘ **drop off:** to bring and leave
> something somewhere;
> opposite = *pick up*

CD 1
Track 28

**B**  Read the statements below. Then listen to each phone call again.
What would the person in each conversation say next? Choose the best answer.

1. a. Yes, eight o'clock is fine. We'll see you then.

   b. No, sorry; but she'll call you back tonight.

   c. Sure. How's 7:30?

2. a. Great. I'll be in this afternoon.

   b. OK, thanks. I'll bring them in today.

   c. No, sorry. That doesn't work for me.

3. a. Yes, there are ten.

   b. Because I need to see the dentist.

   c. I'm sorry, but do you have something later?

4. a. OK, I'll see you at school later.

   b. Sure. I'll pick you up in ten minutes.

   c. Yes, it is.

ASK ANSWER

For what things do you usually make an appointment?

When you go to a restaurant, do you usually make a reservation?

## 3 Pronunciation    Reduced forms of *could you* and *would you*

CD 1
Track 29

**A**  Listen to these sentences. Notice the reduced pronunciation of *could you* and *would you* in each sentence.

1. Could you open the window? It's hot in here.

2. Would you hold the door for me? Thanks.

3. Could you drop me off at school?

4. Would you help me lift this box?

CD 1
Track 30

**B**  Listen to these sentences. Circle the words you hear.

1. That radio is really loud. Could you / Would you turn it down, please?

2. I think the computer is broken. Could you / Would you please look at it?

3. The phone's ringing. Could you / Would you answer it, please?

4. Let me see if he's in his office. Could you / Would you hold for a moment?

**C**  With a partner, practice reading the sentences in **B**. Use reduced forms of *could you* and *would you.*

# 4 Speaking  **I'd like to make an appointment.**

**A**  Listen to the conversation. Then answer the questions with a partner.

1. Why is Minh calling ISS Language Center?

2. When is he planning to go there?

**Martina:** Hello, ISS Language Center. This is Martina.

**Minh:** Yeah, hi. I'm in a TOEFL class that starts next week. I'd like to make an appointment to see the student counselor first.

**Martina:** Sure. I can help you with that. Let's see . . . can you come in tomorrow at 10:30?

**Minh:** No, that time isn't good for me. Do you have anything later in the day?

**Martina:** Let me check. . . . OK, how's 4:15?

**Minh:** That's perfect.

**Martina:** Great. Now, I just need to get your name.

**Minh:** It's Minh Nguyen.

**Martina:** Could you spell your last name for me, please?

**Minh:** Sure, it's N-G-U-Y-E-N.

**B**  Practice the conversation with a partner.

# 5 Speaking Strategy

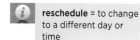

reschedule = to change to a different day or time

| Useful Expressions: Making appointments | | |
|---|---|---|
| **Explaining why you're calling** | | |
| I'm calling to / I'd like to | make an appointment to see a counselor. | |
| | make a dental / doctor's / hair appointment. | |
| | reschedule my appointment / our meeting. | |
| **Scheduling the time** | | |
| **Can you come in** tomorrow at 2:00? | That's perfect. / That works great. | |
| **Can you make it** tomorrow at 2:00? | No, that day / time isn't good for me. | |
| **How's / What about** tomorrow at 4:00? | | |

**A**  With a partner, read the situation below and create a new conversation similar to the one in Speaking. In your dialog, use at least two Useful Expressions.

**Student A:** You want to make an appointment to get a haircut on Thursday afternoon.

**Student B:** You're a hairstylist at a hair salon. The only appointment you have on Thursday is at 11:30 A.M. You have some afternoon appointments on the weekend.

**B**  Switch roles. You and your classmate meet every Tuesday to practice English.

**Student A:** You need to reschedule your meeting for later in the week. Wednesday at 1:00 is best for you, but you can also meet on Friday.

**Student B:** You can only meet on Thursday or Friday after 1:00.

Hi, Alex. What's up?

I'm calling to . . .

## 6 Language Link   Polite requests with modal verbs and *mind*

**A**   Study the chart. Then read the short dialogs below and complete the sentences.

| | Making Requests | | Responding to Requests |
|---|---|---|---|
| informal | **Can / Will** you<br>**Could / Would** you | help me, please? | OK. / Sure, no problem. / I'd be glad to. /<br>Certainly. / Of course.<br>Sorry, but . . . |
| formal | **Would you mind** | helping me, please? | No, not at all. / No, I'd be glad to.<br>Sorry, but . . . |

1. **A:** Would you mind taking the dog for a walk?

   **B:** No, not at all.

   Speaker A's request is more formal in dialog 1 / 2.

   Speaker B says "No, I can't" to Speaker A in dialog 1 / 2.

2. **A:** Could you open the window?

   **B:** Sorry, but I think it's locked.

**B**   Find the error(s) in each dialog and correct them.
Then practice the dialogs with a partner.

1. A: Can you spelling your last name for me, please?

   B: Of course. It's C-U-E-N-D-E.

2. A: The phone's ringing. Would you answer it, please?

   B: Yes, I would.

3. A: I can't go to class today. Could you take notes for me?

   B: No, I'd be glad to.

4. A: Would you mind to do the dishes tonight? I'm tired.

   B: No, not at all.

**C**   Write a request for each situation. Use the words in parentheses.

1. Your roommate is going grocery shopping. (pick up / some milk)

   _____

2. You didn't understand something your teacher said. (repeat / again)

   _____

3. You and your friend are leaving a party. Your friend drove, but you didn't.
   You're really tired. (drive / home)

   _____

**D**   With a partner, take turns making and responding to the requests in **C**.
Refuse (say "no" to) one request and give a reason why.

> Can you pick up
> some milk, please?

> Sorry, but I'm not coming home
> first. I need to run errands. I'm
> afraid the milk will get warm.

# 7 Communication  My *benriya* service

**A**  Read the information below. Then tell a partner: What does a *benriya* do? Do you think it is a good service?

**Need help or have a problem? Hire a *benriya*!**

In Japan, a *benriya* is a person who fixes things, does household chores, and runs errands. *Benriyas* also do other annoying or difficult tasks for you. For example, they can . . .

- break up with your boyfriend or girlfriend
- talk to an angry friend, family member, or neighbor for you
- be your travel partner on a trip
- help you study
- listen to your problems and give you advice

**B**  Work with a partner and create your own *benriya* service.

- What services do you offer (doing housework, running errands, fixing things, etc.)?
- How much do you charge for each service?
- What is your company's name and when do you work?

| Company name: | Price |
|---|---|
| Hours of operation: | |
| **Service** | **Price** |
| 1. | |
| 2. | |
| 3. | |
| 4. | |
| 5. | |

**C**  What things would you pay a *benriya* to do for you? List 2 or 3 ideas below.

**D**  Get together with a new partner. Imagine you are calling his or her *benriya* service. Tell your partner what you need. Find out what he or she charges. Then switch roles.

**A:** Hello, Handy Helpers Service. How can I help you?

**B:** Yes, hello. I'm calling because I want to break up with my boyfriend. I need some help.

**A:** No problem! We can do that for you.

**B:** Great. Could you tell me how much you charge, please?

**E**  Repeat **D** with three other partners. When you finish, ask your partners: Which *benriya* are you going to hire? Why?

# Out and About

## 1   Vocabulary Link   How's your commute?

**A**   Read the question and three responses. Then complete the chart below. Check answers with a partner.

The Question Lady

# The Question Lady wants to know … How's your commute?

**Tara**

I often ride my bike to school. It takes about 25 minutes, but I like the exercise. If I'm running late, then I take the bus so I can get to class on time. By bus, it only takes about ten minutes.

**Felipe**

I live outside of Sao Paulo and I commute into the city every day by car. I'm often stuck in traffic for an hour or more, and that's no fun. For a short time, I took the subway to work, but that was worse. Sure, I could pass the time by sleeping or reading, but the crowded trains were terrible. Driving takes longer, but I prefer it.

**Yoon**

About a year ago, my company moved from Seoul to Pusan so now I've got a really long commute—about 227 km (142 miles). My wife and kids stay in Seoul, and every Monday morning I catch the bullet train to Pusan and spend the week there. On Friday nights, I go back to Seoul and spend time with my family on the weekend.

| You can go or travel somewhere . . . | To go or travel somewhere, you can . . . |
|---|---|
| **by** bike, _____, _____, plane, subway, taxi, train. <br><br> **on** foot. ( = walking) | _____ your bike. <br><br> **drive** your car. <br><br> **catch** / _____ a bus, cab, plane, subway, train. |

**B**   Answer the questions with a partner.

1. How does each person in **A** commute (travel) to and from school or work?

2. Whose commute is the shortest? Whose is the longest?

3. Does it take Tara a long time to take the bus to school?

4. When Felipe took the train, how did he pass the time?

5. Does Yoon spend a lot of time with his family? Why or why not?

6. Your class starts at 10:00 and it's now 9:55. You're still at home. Are you running late or are you on time?

*It takes* + time

It takes 30 minutes to bike to class.

It took 2 hours to do my homework.

It takes a long time to learn a language.

ASK   ANSWER

How do you commute to and from school or work? How long does it take?

## 2 Listening   Commuters around the globe

CD 1
Track 32

**A** You are going to hear the first part of a news report. Read the questions below. Then listen and choose the best answer for each one.

1. The average person's commute is _____ one way.

   a. 40 minutes     b. one hour     c. nearly 2 hours

2. What question is this news show going to answer?

   a. Why are people's commutes getting longer?

   b. Who has the longest commute time in the world?

   c. How do people pass the time while commuting?

CD 1
Track 33

**B** You will hear four people giving an answer to question 2 in **A**. Read the statements below. Then listen and match a statement with a speaker. One statement is extra.

| | |
|---|---|
| Speaker 1 | I make plans for the day. |
| Speaker 2 | I study or phone people. |
| Speaker 3 | I read while I drive. |
| Speaker 4 | I sleep or listen to music. |
| | I listen to stories. |

CD 1
Track 33

**C** How does each person commute to work or school? Listen again and write the type(s) of transportation (bus, subway, bike, car, etc.) each person uses.

Speaker 1: by / on _____

Speaker 2: by / on _____

Speaker 3: by / on _____

Speaker 4: by / on _____

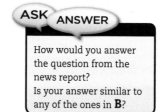

ASK ANSWER

How would you answer the question from the news report?
Is your answer similar to any of the ones in **B**?

## 3 Reading   Surprising neighborhoods

**A** Look at the photos and the names of the cities and neighborhoods on page 53. Then read the statements below. Which neighborhood do you think each sentence describes? In some cases, both answers are possible.

| | | |
|---|---|---|
| 1. To enter this neighborhood, you go through a gate. | Inwood | Fes-al-Bali |
| 2. You can go to this neighborhood by subway. | Inwood | Fes-al-Bali |
| 3. It has an old forest. | Inwood | Fes-al-Bali |
| 4. You can see animals in this neighborhood. | Inwood | Fes-al-Bali |
| 5. You can't drive cars here. | Inwood | Fes-al-Bali |
| 6. It has a university. | Inwood | Fes-al-Bali |
| 7. You can get lost here. | Inwood | Fes-al-Bali |
| 8. Its streets are very narrow. | Inwood | Fes-al-Bali |
| 9. Its streets are usually very crowded. | Inwood | Fes-al-Bali |

**B** Kyle and Farid made web pages about their neighborhoods for a class project. Read about their neighborhoods. Were your answers in **A** correct? Make any necessary changes.

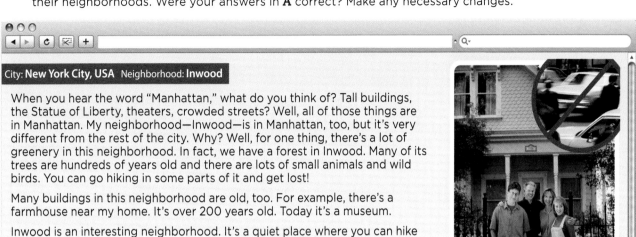

City: **New York City, USA**  Neighborhood: **Inwood**

When you hear the word "Manhattan," what do you think of? Tall buildings, the Statue of Liberty, theaters, crowded streets? Well, all of those things are in Manhattan. My neighborhood—Inwood—is in Manhattan, too, but it's very different from the rest of the city. Why? Well, for one thing, there's a lot of greenery in this neighborhood. In fact, we have a forest in Inwood. Many of its trees are hundreds of years old and there are lots of small animals and wild birds. You can go hiking in some parts of it and get lost!

Many buildings in this neighborhood are old, too. For example, there's a farmhouse near my home. It's over 200 years old. Today it's a museum.

Inwood is an interesting neighborhood. It's a quiet place where you can hike in the parks. But then you can take a subway and, in 20 minutes, you can be in busy midtown Manhattan.

If you're ever in New York City, come and visit Inwood and see a part of Manhattan you didn't know existed. You'll be glad you did!

City: **Fes, Morocco**   Neighborhood: **Fes-al-Bali**

My name is Farid and I live in Fes-al-Bali—a neighborhood in Fes that's over 1,200 years old. You can find everything in my neighborhood—restaurants, shops, cafes, tearooms, and theaters. There are something like 10,000 businesses. We've also got one of the oldest universities in the world—the University of Al-Karaouine. It opened in the year 859.

The whole neighborhood of Fes-al-Bali is surrounded by a high wall with gates. You can drive inside the main gate, but once in, you can only travel through the streets on foot, by bicycle . . . or donkey! In fact, Fes-al-Bali is one of the largest car-free areas in the world. Still, the streets get pretty crowded—mostly because they're very narrow. Oh, and speaking of the streets, there are over 9,000 of them. It takes about 40 minutes to walk from one end of my neighborhood to the other, but be careful—the streets aren't straight. They're very long and winding and it's easy to get lost. Just last week I had to help some tourists from Australia.

If you're ever in Morocco, be sure to spend some time in Fes—and in my neighborhood, Fes-al-Bali. It's a place you'll never forget!

**C** Quickly scan the reading to find what each number describes. Write your answers. The first one is done as an example.

20: *the number of minutes it takes to go from Inwood to midtown Manhattan*

40: _____

200: *the age of* _____

859: _____

1,200: _____

9,000: *the number of* _____

10,000: _____

> **ASK ANSWER**
>
> How are these neighborhoods different from yours?
>
> Which neighborhood would you like to visit? Why?

# 4 Language Link    Intensifiers: *really, very, pretty*

**A**  Study the information in the chart. Then complete the sentences below with *really, very,* and/or *pretty.* Which sentences have more than one answer? Tell a partner.

| | adverb | adverb | |
|---|---|---|---|
| I (don't) talk | really / very | loudly | in class. |
| I talk | pretty | | |

| | | adverb | adjective | noun |
|---|---|---|---|---|
| I (don't) have | a | really / very | long | commute. |
| I have | | pretty | | |

| | adverb | verb | |
|---|---|---|---|
| I (don't) | really | like | my new bike. |

> *Really, very,* and *pretty* make adjectives and adverbs stronger.
>
> *Really* and *very* are stronger than *pretty.*
>
> *Really* can come before a verb. *Very* cannot.

1. I don't know Joan _____ well. Do you?

2. I usually take the subway to work. I don't _____ like to drive.

3. A: Who's that man over there?

   B: I'm _____ sure it's Leo, but I'm not certain.

4. That was a _____ good movie. I loved it.

 You can use "at all" with negatives to mean "zero" or "never":

I **didn't** like that movie **at all**.

**B**  Unscramble the words and make sentences. Then tell a partner: Are the sentences true for you? If they aren't, change them so they are true.

1. busy / I / a / have / pretty / schedule _____

2. live / I / noisy / really / in / neighborhood / a _____

3. don't / movies / really / scary / like / I _____

4. close / family / isn't / my / very _____

5. commute / it's / on / very / crowded / my _____

# 5 Writing    Come to my neighborhood

**A**  Read the paragraphs on the right. Then tell a partner: Where does the writer live? What are the good things about his neighborhood? What are the bad things?

**B**  Think about your neighborhood's good and bad points. Make a list of each. Then write two or three paragraphs about your neighborhood.

**C**  Exchange your writing with a partner. Would you like to live in your partner's neighborhood? Why or why not?

> I live in a busy neighborhood in Seoul called Jamsil. There are good and bad things about living here.
>
> The best thing about my neighborhood is it's convenient. It's pretty easy for me to get to school by subway, bus, or cab. There are also a lot of stores and restaurants in my neighborhood, and there's a big park too. It's a great place to ride your bike or relax and it only takes five minutes to walk there from my house.
>
> The worst thing about my neighborhood is it's really noisy. There are a lot of big apartment buildings and I live on a pretty busy street. It's not the quietest neighborhood in Seoul, but I like living here!

# 6 Communication   Improving your community

**A** Cities around the world have different problems. Read about one city below. Then discuss the questions with a partner.

1. What is the city of Bogota doing? Why?

2. What do you think of the idea? Could it work in your city? Why or why not?

**Problem:** People in cities need open areas to exercise, but often there are too many cars and not enough parks.

**One city's solution:** Every Sunday from 7:00 A.M. to 2:00 P.M., Bogota, Colombia, closes its main city streets to cars and other motor vehicles. People can ride their bikes, walk, skate, play music, and spend time with friends and family on car-free city streets. The event helps people be healthier. Today, other cities around the world, including Melbourne, Australia and Quito, Ecuador, have similar events.

**B** With a partner, think of a problem in your city or neighborhood or choose one from the box below. Then think of at least one solution for the problem and explain why it's a good idea.

- Too many people commute to work or school every day by car.

- Children have no place to get exercise because there are no parks in my neighborhood.

- Your idea: _____

**Problem:** _____

**Our solution:** _____

_____

**Why it's a good idea:** _____

**C** Get together with another pair.

**Pair A:** Present your problem and explain your solution(s).

**Pair B:** Listen to Pair A's ideas. When they finish, answer the question below about their presentation. Explain your opinion to them.

What do you think of Pair A's idea?

❏ I really like the idea because . . .

❏ I kind of like the idea, but . . .

❏ Sorry, but I don't think the idea can work at all because . . .

What is the most bike-friendly city in the world?
a. Amsterdam, Holland
b. Beijing, China
c. San Francisco, USA

**D** Switch roles and repeat **C**.

Check out the World Link video.          Practice your English online at http://elt.heinle.com/worldlink

## 1 Vocabulary Link   Applying to college

**A** Read the posting on the website. Then answer the questions with a partner.

1. What is Kento's problem?

2. Do you think Sergei's advice is good? Why or why not?

---

**Student Forums**                                    **Topic: Choosing a college**

I'm trying to choose a college. My family wants me to go to Tokyo University or Waseda University. They're two of the best colleges in Japan, but there's a lot of competition. Thousands of people apply to these schools every year, but they only admit a couple of hundred. It's a lot of work to get into these schools. And I'm not even sure I want to go to college right now!  It's a really hard decision and I need some help!

   ~Kento (Tokyo, Japan)

Hi, Kento: Some students get accepted to a school, but they're not really ready for university. Here's my recommendation: After graduation from high school, study abroad and improve your language skills, or apply for an internship* for a year. Later, when you're ready for college, you can show how your "year off" prepared you for university. Good luck!

   ~Sergei (Moscow, Russia)

   *internship: a job, usually done for a short time, in which you learn about a certain type of work

---

**B** Complete the chart with a word in blue from **A**. Then use the correct form of a word in the chart to complete the sentences below.

| Verb | Noun |
|------|------|
| _____ | admission |
| _____ (to/for) | application |
| compete | _____ |
| decide | _____ |
| graduate | _____ |
| recommend | _____ |

 The suffixes **-ion, -ation, -ition**, and **-sion** change verbs into nouns.

*graduate + ion = graduation*

*recommend + ation = recommendation*

*compete + ition = competition*

*decide + sion = decision*

1. My brother _____ from Oxford University last year.

2. If you want to go to IES Language School, you can _____ online, or they will mail a(n) _____ to you.

3. These days, there's a lot of _____ for jobs. For one job, we interviewed over 100 people!

4. Leo got into Harvard and Yale, but he can't _____ which university is better.

5. Wesley College _____ students twice a year—you can enter in August or January.

6. I'm new to this neighborhood. Can you _____ a good place to eat?

**ASK ANSWER**

How many universities are you going to (or did you) apply to? Did you get into them?

Can you recommend a good place to study English?

## 2 Listening    Not your typical school

**A**  You're going to hear an interview about a special school. Look at the profile below. Why do you think Stratton Mountain School is special? Tell a partner.

CD 1
Track 34

**B**  A student is going to talk about the school below. Listen and complete the profile. Use only one word per blank.

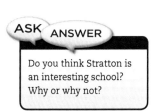

**School Profile**

**Name:** Stratton Mountain School (for students ages _____ to _____)

**Where:** Vermont, USA

**Students:** Most are _____ and snowboarders.

After graduation, many compete in the Winter _____.

**A typical day at Stratton:**

7:00 A.M.: _____

8:00 A.M. to _____: Students are in _____.

12:30 to 5:00 P.M.: Students have _____.

**C**  Review your notes in **B**. Then tell a partner: Why is Stratton an unusual high school?

CD 1
Track 35

**D**  Read sentences 1–3 below. Then listen again. Choose the correct answer for each one.

1. A *coed* school admits . . .
   **A:** boys only.
   **B:** girls only.
   **C:** both boys and girls.

2. A *dorm* is a type of student . . .
   **A:** activity.
   **B:** housing.
   **C:** training.

3. A school's *alumni* are . . .
   **A:** graduates from the school.
   **B:** students now at the school.
   **C:** teachers at the school.

ASK ANSWER

Do you think Stratton is an interesting school? Why or why not?

## 3 Pronunciation    Reduced pronunciation of *going to*

CD 1
Track 36

**A**  Listen to the sentences. Notice the reduced pronunciation of *going to* in each sentence.

1. I'm going to apply to three colleges.

2. He's going to clean the house next week.

3. We're going to study together for the big exam.

4. They're not going to finish in time.

CD 1
Track 37

**B**  Listen to the sentences and write the missing words you hear.

1. _____ meet them before 3:00.
2. _____ take a vacation this summer.
3. _____ call us tomorrow.
4. _____ attend Harvard University.

**C**  Take turns saying the sentences in **A** and **B** with a partner.

## 4 Speaking · **Look on the bright side.**

**CD 1**
**Track 38**

**A** Listen to the conversation. Then answer the questions with a partner.

1. Tom is unhappy about something. What?

2. How does Hans make Tom feel better? Underline Hans's advice.

3. What do you think "look on the bright side" means?

**Hans:** Hey, Tom. How's it going with the college applications?

**Tom:** So-so. I didn't get into McGill University.

**Hans:** Really? Sorry to hear that. Did you apply to any other schools?

**Tom:** Yeah, three others.

**Hans:** And?

**Tom:** I got into all of them.

**Hans:** Well, that's great!

**Tom:** Yeah, but I really wanted to go to McGill.

**Hans:** Well, look on the bright side—three other schools accepted you.

**Tom:** Yeah, I guess you're right.

**Hans:** So, which school are you going to attend?

**Tom:** I'm not sure. Maybe I'll go to Queen's University.

**B** Practice the conversation with a partner.

## 5 Speaking Strategy

| Useful Expressions: Offering another point of view | |
|---|---|
| **I didn't get accepted to McGill University.** | |
| Look on the bright side . . .<br>Well, the good news is . . .<br>Look at it this way . . .<br>Yes, but on the other hand . . .<br>(Yes, but) then again . . . | three other schools accepted you. |

**A** Read the problems. For each, add one more "positive" point of view to the chart.

| The problem | A positive point of view |
|---|---|
| You applied to two English schools: one in the UK and one in Australia. You really wanted to study in the UK, but only the school in Australia accepted you. | 1. You got accepted to a good school.<br>2. _____ |
| You're invited to a party at the beach. You're not sure if you want to go. You're worried you won't know many people. | 1. You can meet new people.<br>2. _____ |

**B** Choose one situation from **A**. With a partner, create a short conversation like the one in Speaking. Use the Useful Expressions in your dialog.

**C** Change roles. Use the other situation and repeat **B**.

# 6 Language Link    **Plans and decisions with *be going to* and *will***

**A**  Read these conversations. Then complete sentences 1 and 2 below.

Ana:    I got accepted to college.

Pablo:  Congratulations!

Ana:    Thanks. I'm going to attend McGill University in the fall.

Yuri:      I want to register for the grammar class.

Advisor:  I'm sorry. That class is full.

Yuri:      OK. I'll register for the writing class, then.

1. Ana uses *be going to* to talk about . . .

☐ a. a sudden decision.

☐ b. a plan she already made.

2. Yuri uses *will* ('ll) to talk about . . .

☐ a. a sudden decision.

☐ b. a plan he already made.

**B**  Complete the sentences with *be going to* or *will*. Then check your answers with a partner.

1. I graduate from high school in June. Then I _____ attend college in the fall.

2. I'm bored and don't know what to do. Wait, I know . . . I _____ read and watch TV.

3. Waiter: What would you like today?
   Customer: Let's see . . . I _____ have the chicken and rice, please.

4. I bought my ticket last month. I _____ visit Paris from July 1 to July 14.

5. A:  This box is too heavy!
   B:  Wait! I _____ help you.

**C**  Read what these new students are planning to do. Make sentences using *be (not) going to* with a partner.

Carlos

Ariana

Max and Sara

☐ live at home
☐ apply for scholarships
☐ study business

☐ major in law
☐ live in the dorms
☐ go to a large university

☐ live in student housing
☐ study together
☐ work part-time

> *Carlos is going to live at home. He's not going to apply for scholarships.*

**ASK  ANSWER**

What about you? What are your future plans for school or work?

# 7 Communication    Find someone who . . .

**A**   The two questions in the chart ask about someone's future plans. Read the answers. Then complete each question with *be going to*. Check answers with a partner.

| *yes / no* questions | _____ **study** English this summer? | Yes, I am. / Maybe. / No, I'm not. |
| *wh-* questions | What _____ **do** after graduation? | I'm going to take a trip. |

**B**   Read the questions on the left side of the chart. In the "Me" column, check ( ✔ ) the activities you're planning to do in the future. Then add your own question.

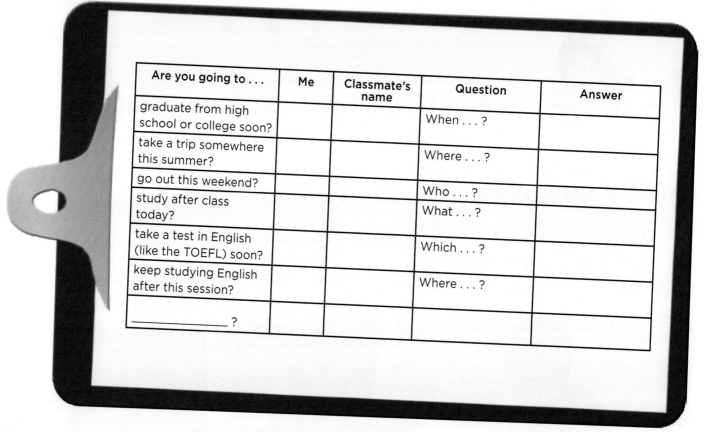

| Are you going to . . . | Me | Classmate's name | Question | Answer |
|---|---|---|---|---|
| graduate from high school or college soon? | | | When . . . ? | |
| take a trip somewhere this summer? | | | Where . . . ? | |
| go out this weekend? | | | Who . . . ? | |
| study after class today? | | | What . . . ? | |
| take a test in English (like the TOEFL) soon? | | | Which . . . ? | |
| keep studying English after this session? | | | Where . . . ? | |
| _____ ? | | | | |

**C**   Interview your classmates. For each question, find a different person who answers *yes*. Write the classmate's name. Ask another question to get more details.

Yes, I am.

Next month.

Are you going to graduate from college soon?

When are you going to graduate?

**D**   Look at the answers you got in **C**. Which one was the most interesting? Tell the class.

# Student Life

## Lesson B  After graduation

## 1  Vocabulary Link  One of these days . . .

**A**  Read about these two people. Then answer the questions with a partner.

1. What is each person planning to do in the future? When is he or she planning to do it?

2. Which person has more of a definite plan about his or her future?

I'm going to graduate the day after tomorrow. I'm finishing school, but I've already got lots of plans for the future. This summer, for example, I'm going to study for the medical school exam. Next year, I hope to enter medical school, and someday, I plan to be a doctor.

Carmen

I'm going to graduate in two weeks. I'm a little nervous because after graduation, I don't have any clear plans. I'd like to take a short vacation in the near future—maybe next month. Sooner or later, I also need to get a job, but I don't know what I want to do exactly. I'm sure I'll make a decision—one of these days.

Gabe

**B**  Complete the chart with the blue time expressions in **A**.

| Future Time Expressions | |
|---|---|
| **Talk about a definite (specific) time** | **Talk about an indefinite (uncertain) time** |
| tomorrow | soon |
| the _____ | **in** a few days |
| **in** two hours / days / _____ / months / years | **in** the_____ |
| **next** week / _____ / _____ | _____ |
| **this** _____ / spring / fall / winter | someday / one _____ |
| _____ graduation / school / work | |

**C**  Complete the sentences. Then check your answers with a partner.

1. If today is Thursday, *the day after tomorrow* is _____.

2. It's 2:00. You say, "I'll be home *in two hours*." You'll be home at _____:00.

3. It's May. You say, "I'm going to graduate *next June*." This means you're going to graduate next month / in 13 months.

4. It's May. You say, "I'm going to graduate *this June*." This means you're going to graduate next month / in 13 months.

5. Your friend says, "We should have coffee *one of these days*." He or She is / isn't making an appointment with you.

6. If you tell a friend, "I'm going to Jamaica *in a few days*," you are / aren't going to Jamaica very soon.

**D**  Are you going to do any of these things in the future? When? Tell a partner.

complete this English class          have children          take a trip somewhere          see my friends

## 2 Listening    Career Day

**A**   Look at the photos. What are the people doing? How do you prepare for these activities?

a written exam

a physical exam

CD 1
Track 39

**B**   You're going to hear an ad for Career Day. Read the questions. Then listen and check the correct answers.

1. Who is Career Day for?    ☐ students    ☐ teachers    ☐ parents
2. What is another word for *career*?    ☐ school    ☐ child    ☐ job

CD 1
Track 40

**C**   Listen to Jeff, a speaker at Career Day, describe a process. Put the steps in order from 1 to 5. Then complete the sentence.

_____ take a written exam     _____ take final exams     _____ go to school for four months

_____ take training courses     _____ take a physical exam

Jeff is going to be a _____.

> **ASK** **ANSWER**
>
> Jeff completed all the steps in **C**. Which step would be the hardest for you? Why?

## 3 Reading    An opportunity of a lifetime

**A**   The people below are talking about Stephanie. Read what they say.
What do you think Stephanie is going to do this summer? Share with a partner.

Mrs. Lee, mother

*She's going to travel alone for six months. It's a great opportunity!*

Mr. Lee, father

*This is a perfect job for her. She loves to take photos and meet new people.*

*After she finishes her work assignment, I'm going to meet her in Europe.*

Tommy Farr, boyfriend

**B**   Now read the web page. Was your guess about Stephanie's summer plans correct?

| NEWS | UPDATE | PHOTOS | CONTACT US |

**We now have a winner! Stephanie Lee from Vancouver, Canada, answered our questions and won the top prize: she's going to be our youth travel reporter in Europe! A week after college graduation, Stephanie starts her six-month travel adventure. She'll write about her experiences for our World Link website. Here were some of Stephanie's answers to our questions:**

**Do you have any international travel experience and what does this tell us about you?**
Yes, I do. Two years ago, I spent the summer in Hong Kong. I stayed with my grandmother and worked in the family business. I also visited Africa last year. I think this shows that I'm self-sufficient—I can do things on my own—and that I'm not afraid of new experiences.

In Africa, I went to Tanzania. The highlight was climbing Mount Kilimanjaro. It's the highest mountain in Africa. The climb was very hard. Two people turned back before they reached the top. I made it all the way! Once I start something, I never give up.

**What do you think will be the hardest part of this job?**
I'm going to be visiting over 25 countries where people speak lots of different languages so communicating with others might be difficult sometimes. I speak some French and German, and English, of course. I'll also be traveling with a translator in many places so I'm sure that will help. I'm also sure that sooner or later, I'm going to miss my family and friends. It's normal. But I also know from experience that this feeling will pass—especially when you meet new people.

**Why should we choose you?**
Because I love to travel and meet new people. I'm also a hard worker and will have no trouble filing reports on time. I'm always very punctual!

Stephanie

**C**  Find a word or phrase in the text that has the same meaning as the words below.

1. independent _____

2. quit _____

3. speaking _____

4. lively, with a lot of energy _____

**D**  Complete the sentences about Stephanie's new job with words from the box.
(You will not use all the words.)

| Africa | punctual | school | reporter | translator |
| photographing | Europe | popular | talking to | website |

1. Stephanie Lee is going to spend her summer in _____.

2. She's going to work as a _____ for a _____.

3. The hardest part of the job will probably be _____ new people.

4. Stephanie is perfect for the job because she's very _____.

ASK ANSWER

1. Look at answer 4 in **D**. What other reasons is Stephanie perfect for the job?

2. Would you like to do Stephanie's job? Why or why not?

# 4 Language Link    Predictions with *be going to* and *will*

**A** People use *be going to* and *will* to make predictions (guesses about the future). Look at the pictures and read the captions. Then complete sentences 1 and 2 with *be going to* or *will*.

I'm sure you're going to be very successful.
*or*
I'm sure you'll be very successful.

"Look! That truck is going to go through that red light!"

1. In picture A, the man is making a general prediction about the student's future, so he can use _____ or _____.

2. In picture B, we can see that the action is happening now or very soon, so we use _____ but not _____.

**B** The sentences below all make predictions. Complete each with *be going to, will,* or *both*. Then explain your answer choices to a partner.

1. Liam did really well in college. I'm sure he _____ get a good job.

2. I think you _____ like this movie. It's a comedy and you like funny movies.

3. The score is 5 to 1 and there's only one minute left in the game. Our team _____ lose for sure.

4. Scientists now believe there _____ be nine billion people on Earth by the year 2040.

5. Look at those dark clouds. It _____ rain soon.

**C** Study the information in the chart. Then read the predictions below. Do you think each one will happen? Why or why not? Tell a partner.

| Making predictions about the future | | |
|---|---|---|
| Leo studied hard. | **I'm sure / I bet** | he's going to / he'll <u>pass</u> the test. |
| Mona didn't study. | | she isn't going to / she won't <u>pass</u> the test. |

- It's common to use *I'm sure* and *I bet* to make a prediction you are certain about.
- Use *probably* or *maybe* when you aren't 100% sure about your prediction:
  He'll <u>probably</u> pass the test.
  She <u>probably</u> won't pass the test.
  <u>Maybe</u> we'll find a cure for cancer someday.

1. We'll find life on other planets.

2. Scientists will cure diseases like AIDS and cancer.

3. Newspapers and magazines will disappear.
   All information will be online.

> In the near future, we'll probably find life on other planets . . .

> Really? Maybe it'll happen, but not in the near future . . .

## 5 Writing  **My life now and in the future**

**A**  Use the topics below or ones of your own. First, write about what you are doing now. Then write about your future. Use *be going to* and *will* to make predictions.

> family    job    travel    school    love life

> **My Life Now and in the Future**
> Right now, I'm taking an English class.
> I'm working part-time at a cafe.
> I live at home with my parents and two brothers. I have a boyfriend.
>   Someday, I'm going to get married and live in a house by the ocean. Sooner or later, I'll . . .

**B**  Exchange papers with a partner. Do you think your partner's predictions will come true?

## 6 Communication  **Predicting the future**

**A**  Read this profile of Prince William.
With a partner, make some predictions about his future.

**Birthday:**     June 21, 1982
**Schooling:**    He attended university at St. Andrews in Scotland. He studied art history. After graduation, he also lived and worked for a short time in Chile, Belize, and parts of Africa. He is now a pilot with the Royal Air Force.
**Hobbies:**      He loves sports, including rugby, hockey, swimming, skiing, and running. He likes to listen to music.
**Personality:**  He is shy in public. In private, he is strong-willed and independent.

> Someday, he's probably going to be the King of England.

> I bet he'll marry someone famous, too, like a movie star.

**B**  Now complete your own personal profile.

**Schooling:**

**Hobbies:**

**Personality:**

**C**  Exchange profiles with a partner. Make predictions about your partner's job, travel, school, family, and love life.

> I think you're going to get a good job someday. And you'll probably also . . .

  Check out the World Link video.        Practice your English online at http://elt.heinle.com/worldlink

# Review: Units 4-6

## 1 Storyboard

 **A** Ruben is talking to his teacher, Gina Walker. Complete the conversations. Then tell a partner: Why does Ruben want to talk to Professor Walker?

Later in Ms. Walker's office . . .

 **B** Practice the conversation with a partner. Then change roles and practice again.

# 2 See It and Say It

**A** Look at the neighborhood and discuss the questions with a partner.

- What household chores and errands can you see people doing?

- What are other people in the picture doing?

- Do you think this neighborhood is a good place to live? Why or why not?

- Is this neighborhood similar to or different from yours? Explain your answer.

**B** Do the following:

**Student A:** Where is a good place for people to meet or relax in your neighborhood? Tell your partner.

**Student B:** Imagine you want to go to this place. Ask your partner to . . .

- give you directions from school.

- tell you how long it takes to get there.

**C** Switch roles and do **B** again.

> How can I get to Bix's Cafe from here?

> Take Bus 211 to . . .

## 3 I Need Your Advice!

**A** Read sentences 1-6. What advice would you give to someone who made these statements? Think about your answers.

1. I'm always running late.

2. I forgot to bring today's English homework and it's 25% of the class grade.

3. My parents don't like my friends.

4. I have a terrible commute. It takes over two hours every day.

5. I get really nervous when I have to talk to others in English.

6. I bought a new cell phone and it's not working.

 **B** Get into a group of three people. Write the numbers 1 to 6 on six small pieces of paper. Put the numbers in a bag or hat.

- When it's your turn, choose a number. Read aloud the problem in **A** that goes with your number. Explain the problem in more detail.

- Your partners will listen and give you advice.

- Think about their suggestions. Which person gave you the best advice? Why?

## 4 *Be going to* or *Will?*

**A** The chart shows the different uses of *be going to* and *will*. Complete the sentences below with *be going to*, *will*, or both.

|  | to talk about plans you already made | to talk about a sudden decision | to talk about an action that is about to happen | to make a general prediction about the future |
|---|---|---|---|---|
| *be going to* | ✓ |  | ✓ | ✓ |
| *will* |  | ✓ |  | ✓ |

1. I decided to take the TOEFL exam. I _____ take it next spring.

2. It's a beautiful evening. I think I _____ take a walk.

3. The score is 10 to 1 and there's a minute left in the game. Our team _____ lose for sure.

4. I bet there _____ be thousands of people at the free concert in the park tomorrow.

5. What _____ do this weekend? Do you have any plans?

6. A: The two o'clock movie is sold out, but we still have seats for the four o'clock show.
   B: OK, I _____ take two tickets for the 4:00 show.

7. Hurry! Class starts in two minutes. We _____ be late!

8. She's really smart. I bet she _____ get accepted to a good school.

 **B** Compare your answers with a partner's. Explain why you chose *be going to*, *will*, or both in **A**.

# 5 Listening

**A** Read the poll below and choose your answer. Then take a class vote.
What was the most common answer in your class?

### POLL:
Do you think you'll get married?
a. Yes, definitely. I want to get married.
b. Yes, maybe someday, but I'm not sure when.
c. No, never. Marriage isn't for me.

CD 1
Track 41

**B** A magazine asked a group of university students for their opinions on different topics.
Listen and put the charts in the order (1-4) you hear them talked about.

_____

yes  no

_____

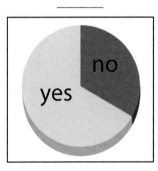

no
yes

_____

60

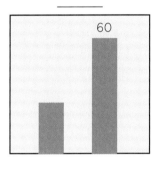

_____

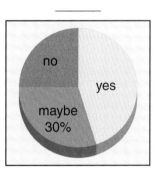

no
yes
maybe
30%

CD 1
Track 41

**C** Listen again and label the parts of each chart in **B** with the correct numbers / percentages.
Some numbers will not be given. You have to guess them.

**D** Look at your answers (1–4) in **B**. What do the students interviewed think?
Read the sentences below and then choose the correct answer.

Chart 1: Most / Some of the students think it's OK for couples with children to get divorced.

Chart 2: This year, a couple / more of them think studying abroad is good.

Chart 3: Most / Half of them think the university entrance exam is too difficult.

Chart 4: A lot / Almost none of them think plastic surgery is OK.

 **plastic surgery:** a medical operation that changes or improves your looks

**E** What do you think about the four opinions in **D**?
Compare your ideas with a partner's. Explain your reasons.

I think it's OK for couples
with kids to get divorced.

Sorry, but I don't agree . . .

# Combo Split

# World Link
## Developing English Fluency

# 2A

HEINLE
CENGAGE Learning™

Australia • Brazil • Japan • Korea • Mexico • Singapore • Spain • United Kingdom • United States

**HEINLE**
CENGAGE Learning™

**World Link Combo Split 2A**
**2nd Edition**

Publisher: Sherrise Roehr

Senior Development Editor:
Margarita Matte

Senior Development Editor:
Jennifer Meldrum

Senior Development Editor:
Katherine Carroll

Director of Global Marketing:
Ian Martin

Senior Product Marketing Manager:
Katie Kelley

Assistant Marketing Manager:
Anders Bylund

Content Project Manager:
John Sarantakis

Senior Print Buyer:
Mary Beth Hennebury

Composition: PreMediaGlobal

Cover/Text Design: Page2 LLC

Cover Image: iStockphoto

**Heinle**
20 Channel Center Street
Boston, MA 02210
USA

Cengage Learning is a leading provider of customized learning solutions with office locations around the globe, including Singapore, the United Kingdom, Australia, Mexico, Brazil, and Japan. Locate our local office at
**international.cengage.com/region**

Cengage Learning products are represented in Canada by Nelson Education, Ltd.

Visit Heinle online at **elt.heinle.com**
Visit our corporate website at **cengage.com**

PHOTO CREDITS: Unit 1: page 2: Luis Sandoval Mandujano/erlucho/iStockphoto.com; page 5: Apollofoto/Used under license from www.shutterstock.com; page 7: center right, Hemera Photo Objects; bottom center, Photodisc; bottom right, Hemera Photo Objects. Unit 2: page 13: PhotoDisc, Inc. Digital Imagery © copyright 2005 PhotoDisc, Inc. Unit 3: page 19: left, Ionescu Ilie Cristian, 2010/Used under license from www.shutterstock.com; right, Michael Ledray, 2010/Used under license from www.shutterstock.com. Unit 5: page 27: Rob Marmion, 2010/Used under license from www.shutterstock.com; page 30: Isaak, 2010/Used under license from www.shutterstock.com. Unit 6: page 36: left, Flashon Studio, 2010/Used under license from www.shutterstock.com; center, Stephen Coburn, 2010/Used under license from www.shutterstock.com; right, Jason Stitt, 2010/Used under license from www.shutterstock.com; page 37: Lucian Coman, 2010/Used under license from www.shutterstock.com

Printed in the United States of America
1 2 3 4 5 6 7 8 9 10 - 14 13 12 11 10

# Scope & Sequence

# All About Me

**Lesson A** The people in my life

## 1 Vocabulary Workout

**A** Who is Linda talking to? Fill in the blanks with words from the box.

| an acquaintance | a close friend | a date | a coworker |
| --- | --- | --- | --- |

1. There's something I need to tell you. It's something I can't even tell my boyfriend.

   *She's talking to* _____.

2. Could you check this letter for me before I give it to the boss?

   *She's talking to* _____.

3. I remember meeting you at Jack's party, but I can't remember your name.

   *She's talking to* _____.

4. I'm sorry. I can't go out with you tonight. I have to work. What about Friday night?

   *She's talking to* _____.

5. We should stop talking and get back to work.

   *She's talking to* _____.

6. We have gone out together for six months. I told my parents about you. They want to meet you.

   *She's talking to* _____.

**B** Who are they? Complete the chart with the names of people in your life.

| | |
| --- | --- |
| Coworkers | _____  _____ |
| Acquaintances | _____  _____ |
| Dates | _____  _____ |
| Close friends | _____  _____ |
| People I went out with, but now we're just friends | _____  _____ |

# 2 Conversation Workout

**A**  Read these introductions.

1. **A:** Hello, Michelle. I'd like you to meet Susan Chang.

    **B:** It's nice to meet you, Susan.

    **C:** It's nice to meet you too, Michelle.

2. **A:** Dave, this is my sister, Graciela.

    **B:** Hi, Graciela. Nice to meet you.

    **C:** Nice to meet you, too.

    Circle the more formal introduction. Write the words or phrases that make it formal.

    _____

**B**  Write conversations.

1. Introduce your best friend to a famous person.

    **You:** _____

    **Famous person** (_____): _____

    **Friend** (_____): _____

2. Introduce a classmate to a member of your family.

    **You:** _____

    **Family member** (_____): _____

    **Classmate** (_____): _____

3. Introduce your teacher to your friend.

    **You:** _____

    **Friend** (_____): _____

    **Teacher** (_____): _____

# 3 Language Workout

**A** Richard is a teacher, but now he's on vacation. Look at the pictures and write sentences about Richard using the simple present or the present continuous.

| **Usually** | **Today** |
|---|---|
| Richard _____ | He _____ |
| He _____ | He _____ |
| He _____ | He _____ |
| He _____ | He _____ |

**B** Complete each sentence with the correct form of the verb in parentheses. Use the simple present or the present continuous.

1. Sorry, I can't talk to you right now. I (be) _____ late for work.

2. Kevin (not, like) _____ loud music.

3. Don't turn off the TV! I (watch) _____ a great movie.

4. Sarah usually (play) _____ tennis with her friends on Saturday.

5. I (study) _____ English now. I (study) _____ every day for an hour after class.

6. This basketball game is really exciting—my team (win) _____ by only two points!

7. Usually, my mother (cook) _____ dinner, but today my brother (cook) _____ for us.

8. Jason (not, drink) _____ coffee. He (like) _____ tea.

**C** Find the mistake in each sentence. Cross it out and correct it.

1. Luis speaks Spanish at home, but now he is speak English.

2. Do you listening to me?

3. We usually are having a lot of homework in this class.

4. Right now Irena writes an e-mail to her family.

# 1  Vocabulary and Language Workout

**A**  Match each sentence starter with the correct ending.

| | |
|---|---|
| 1. I am studying so that I will _____ | a. need a tutor. |
| 2. I can't study because I _____ | b. prepare for the tests. |
| 3. I can't understand this lesson. I _____ | c. get a good grade. |
| 4. If you don't study, you will _____ | d. meet on Friday afternoons. |
| 5. You can learn how to sing beautifully if you _____ | e. take a music class. |
| | f. fail the exam. |
| 6. To get good grades, you need to _____ | g. have basketball practice. |
| 7. If you don't fail an exam, you _____ | h. pass it. |
| 8. The school clubs all _____ | |

**B**  Complete the paragraph with the correct past tense verbs. Use the verbs in the box.

be     move     find     live     want     get     go     finish

When Chang was young, his family (1.) _____ in a

small town. Later they (2.) _____ to Shanghai.

Chang (3.) _____ a good education there.

He (4.) _____ to become a computer programmer.

He (5.) _____ college when he was 20 years old. Then

he (6.) _____ to New York City to find a job. Chang

(7.) _____ very lucky and got a job right away. He

also (8.) _____ a cheap apartment, which was also very

lucky. Chang invited his parents to visit him, but it's too far for them

to travel.

# 2 Reading and Writing

**A** Answer these questions.

1. Do you save a lot of old photos and papers? _____

2. Why or why not? _____

3. Where do you keep your old photos and papers? _____

**B** Read this magazine article about a new hobby.

**+ HOBBIES +**

# Making Memories

**A popular new hobby is scrapbooking—making beautiful books to hold special memories. Scrapbook pages can include photos, drawings, and journal entries. It's not hard to make a scrapbook that you will enjoy for many years. Here are the steps.**

**1.** Choose a theme for your scrapbook pages. Some examples: "School days," "Family travel," "Memories of my grandparents," "Baby's first year."

**2.** Select photos for each page. Two or three really good photos are better than ten so-so photos.

**3.** Find other paper keepsakes to use with your photos. Look for old newspaper clippings, postcards, tickets, report cards, letters—anything made of paper. Use your imagination!

**4.** Design the pages. Put photos and keepsakes together on each page and move them around until you find a layout that you like.

**5.** Glue your photos and keepsakes into place. Then decorate your pages with felt pens, paint, and stickers. Use your imagination!

**6.** Label your pages. This is the most important step! Remember to write down the "5 Ws" of your photos: Who, What, Where, When, and Why. This will make your scrapbook much more interesting and valuable in the future.

**C** Find this information in the article.

1. the definition of *scrapbooking* _____

2. examples of keepsakes _____

3. important things to write on pages _____

4. subjects for a scrapbook _____

5. how to make the pages beautiful _____

**D** Complete the paragraph. Use the past tense of the verbs in parentheses.

At the age of thirteen, I (1. take) _____ my first trip alone. I (2. go) _____ to visit my grandparents in Los Angeles. I (3. feel) _____ very nervous about traveling so far, but my mother (4. say) _____, "Don't worry. You'll be fine." I (5. get) _____ on the airplane and (6. talk) _____ for a long time to a very nice woman who (7. sit) _____ next to me. My grandparents (8. meet) _____ me at the airport and (9. take) _____ me to their home. I (10. stay) _____ there for two weeks, and I (11. have) _____ so much fun with them! It (12. be) _____ my first time in Los Angeles, and I (13. see) _____ lots of really interesting places. In the end, I (14. not, want) _____ to go home!

**E** Write about your own happy memory.

# 2 Let's Eat!

## Lesson A Foods we like

## 1 Vocabulary Workout

**A** Unscramble these adjectives that describe food.

| | |
|---|---|
| 1. tutryeb _buttery_ | 6. ucnyrch _____ |
| 2. ycpsi _____ | 7. ijuyc _____ |
| 3. hayleth _____ | 8. yrcips _____ |
| 4. tewes _____ | 9. rosu _____ |
| 5. dreif _____ | 10. talys _____ |

**B** Label the pictures with words from activity A.

_____

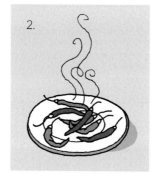

_____

_____

_____

# 2 Conversation Workout

**A** Unscramble the sentences to form suggestions.

1. movie / a / how / tonight / going / to / about

_____?

2. ice cream / why / class / don't / we / after / have / some

_____?

3. about / restaurant / how / the / Italian / new

_____?

4. don't / meet / why / 8:00 / we / at

_____?

5. playing / how / tennis / tomorrow / about

_____?

**B** Number the sentences to make a conversation.

_____ You're right. It's very oily.

_____ OK! Why don't we go to Chicken Paradise?

_____ Well, how about Salad Heaven?

_____ That's a great idea. Their food is much healthier.

_____ Would you like to go out for dinner tonight?

_____ I'm sorry, but I don't like their chicken. It's too greasy.

**C** What would you like to do tonight? Write a similar conversation between you and a friend. Use *Would you . . .* and *How about . . .*

| | |
|---|---|
| **You:** | *Would you . . .* _____ |
| **Your friend:** | _____ |
| **You:** | _____ |
| **Your friend:** | _____ |
| **You:** | _____ |
| **Your friend:** | _____ |

# 3 Language Workout

**A** Write sentences with the comparative form of these adjectives. Use your own ideas.

**Example:** phone calls / letters / nice

_Letters are nicer than phone calls._

1. cats / dogs / friendly _____
2. computer games / chess / difficult _____
3. Mexico City / Tokyo / interesting _____
4. fried chicken / French fries / greasy _____
5. swimming / lying on the beach / relaxing _____
6. cookies / donuts / sweet _____
7. cleaning the house / cooking / hard _____
8. sharks / snakes / dangerous _____
9. (Your own idea) _____
10. (Your own idea) _____

**B** Write sentences with the superlative form of these adjectives.

**Example:** exciting / sport in the Olympics

_I think skiing is the most exciting sport in the Olympics._

1. beautiful / place in our country

_____

2. good / restaurant in our town

_____

3. great / athlete in the world

_____

4. interesting / program on TV now

_____

5. big / problem in the world today

_____

6. quiet / place in our town

_____

# 1   Vocabulary and Language Workout

**A**   Complete the paragraph with words from the box.

| | | | |
|---|---|---|---|
| cut back on | strict diet | increase | diet |
| habits | plenty of | eliminate | lifestyle |

Last week my uncle took me to the most expensive restaurant in town.
I am on a (1.) _____ so I wasn't planning on eating a lot.
My eating (2.) _____ aren't always so good, and lately I have
been trying to (3.) _____ unhealthy foods from my
(4.) _____. I am trying to (5.) _____ greasy foods and
(6.) _____ the amount of fruits and vegetables I eat. However,
my uncle isn't interested in a healthy (7.) _____. He eats lots
of meat and (8.) _____ sweets. I tried to enjoy the meal, but it
wasn't easy.

**B**   Match each sentence starter with the correct ending.

| | |
|---|---|
| 1. When we have food in a restaurant, we _____ | a. have a balanced diet. |
| 2. When we eat a variety of healthy foods, we _____ | b. benefits. |
| 3. Some foods _____ | c. eat out. |
| 4. A slow food diet has health _____ | d. increase our weight. |
| 5. Greasy foods usually _____ | e. protect us against disease. |

**C**   Answer these questions. Use your own information.

1. What kinds of healthy foods do you like?

_____

2. What kinds of unhealthy foods do you like?

_____

3. What good eating habits do you try to follow?

_____

4. What are some benefits of a healthy diet?

_____

# 2  Reading and Writing

**A**  Answer these questions.

1. What are some spicy foods? _____

2. Do you like any of these foods? _____

3. Which countries are famous for spicy food? _____

4. Do you think spicy food is good for your health? _____

   Why or why not? _____

**B**  Now read this Web page.

http://www.foodfacts.*net/chileppers.html

INBOX    ◄✉ REPLY    ◄✉ REPLY ALL    ✉► FORWARD    ✗ DELETE

## Hot, hotter, hottest! Surprising facts about chile peppers

**(1)** Chile peppers are one of the oldest food **crops** in the world. Farmes grew the first chile peppers more than 9,000 years ago.

**(2)** The first chile peppers probably grew in Bolivia. From there, the plant **spread** through South America and the Caribbean. Christopher Columbus brought the filst chile peppers to Europe.

**(3)** The heat in the chile comes from a chemical called capsaicin. Capsaicin has no smell or flavor, but it makes your mouth feel "hot."

**(4)** Scientists believe that chile peppers are a very healthy food because they **are rich in** vitamins. Research shows that chiles do not **damage** the stomach, and Indian scientists discovered that eating chiles can help people lose weight.

**(5)** Indian food is **well-known** for using lots of chile peppers, but Thai food is spicier. The average person in Thailand eats five grams of chile pepper every day—the most in the world!

**(6)** The Aztec Indians of Mexico loved chile peppers so much that they gave them to their king as a gift.

**(7)** The hottest chile pepper in the world is the habanero. It is bright orange and grows in the Caribbean.

**(8)** There are chile sauce factories on every **continent** except Antarctica.

**C**  Match the words from the reading with their meanings.

1. crop _____        a. hurt                4. continent _____     d. famous

2. spread _____      b. move over an area   5. are rich in _____   e. large land area

3. damage _____      c. farm plant          6. well-known _____    f. have many

**D**  Circle true (T) or false (F) and write the number of the section where you found the answers.

1. Mexicans eat the most chile peppers of any people in the world.    T    F    _____

2. Chiles are hot because they have capsaicin in them.    T    F    _____

3. You can find chile sauce factories in Antarctica.    T    F    _____

4. The first chile peppers grew in Europe.    T    F    _____

5. Thai food is spicier than Indian food.    T    F    _____

6. Chile peppers can be dangerous for your health.    T    F    _____

**E** Read the paragraph and circle the correct words.

I'm from Korea, and kimchi is the (1.) *famous / most famous* food from my country. It's made from vegetables, chile peppers, garlic, and salt. Its flavor is sour, salty, and (2.) *spicy / spicier*. The (3.) *most popular / popularest* kind of kimchi is made from cabbage, but there are many other kinds. White kimchi doesn't have chile peppers, so it's (4.) *milder / the most mild*. The (5.) *most spicy / spiciest* kind of kimchi is made from radishes. Kimchi is (6.) *the most healthy / healthier* than other vegetable dishes because it has more vitamins. I love kimchi, and I eat it every day. Some people don't like it, but I think they should try some different kinds. In my opinion, cucumber kimchi is the (7.) *more delicious / most delicious*.

**F** Write about a famous dish from your country. What is it made from? How does it taste? Do you like it? Why or why not? Do other people like it? Use your dictionary for help with new vocabulary.

_____
_____
_____
_____
_____
_____
_____
_____
_____
_____

# 3 Unsolved Mysteries

## Lesson A  What a coincidence!

## 1  Vocabulary Workout

**A**  Solve this crossword puzzle.

### Down

1. not on purpose
2. become friends again
4. go away from each other
5. a fortunate outcome
8. the opposite of unlucky

### Across

3. not be able to do something
6. do something _____ purpose
7. work _____ a solution
9. allow yourself to do something you're not sure about

## 2  Conversation Workout

**A**  Who did it? Write one sentence with each of these words or expressions.

**Example:** likely

_It's likely the cat ate the fish._

1. doubt

_____

2. bet

_____

3. unlikely

_____

4. not seem possible

_____

5. good chance

_____

**B**  What will the woman do or not do? Write sentences with the expressions from activity A.

1. _____
2. _____
3. _____

**C**  What do you think? Complete the conversations with your own ideas. Use the expressions above.

Do you think UFOs are real?

_____
_____

Do you think our country will win ten gold medals in the next Olympics?

_____
_____

Do you think we will have any English homework this week?

_____
_____

# 3 Language Workout

**A** Find at least three stative verbs in this paragraph. List them here.

_____

_____

_____

I love to camp! It's my favorite way to spend my vacation. Every year, my family and I camp in a national park. We sleep in a tent and hike every day. I like to cook over a fire, and the food always tastes wonderful. For a whole week, I see lovely scenery and smell fresh air. At night, I hear the wind blow in the trees, and I feel so peaceful. It doesn't cost much to camp, and I believe it's the best way to appreciate the beauty of our country.

**B** Complete the sentences with the simple present or the present continuous form of the verb in parentheses.

1. Mmm! That pizza (smell) _____ so good!

2. Please don't talk to me now. I (do) _____ my homework.

3. Right now, we (know) _____ several hundred English words.

4. Miguel says he won the lottery, but I (not, believe) _____ him.

5. I (hate) _____ hot weather because I always (feel) _____ tired.

6. Fred (learn) _____ how to cook. His mother (teach) _____ him.

7. I (own) _____ a car, but today I (take) _____ the bus to work.

8. Carol and Aisha (belong) _____ to the International Club.

9. Our teacher (look) _____ angry. I wonder why.

10. This exercise (seem) _____ really easy. I (understand) _____ all of the sentences!

**C** Mark the sentence correct (C) or incorrect (I). Cross out the mistakes and correct them.

1. Sorry, but I'm not understand that word. _____

2. Right now, we look at photos from our vacation. _____

3. Rose and Jennie are listening to a new CD. _____

4. I think that English is a very useful language. _____

5. The onion soup is tasting too salty. _____

6. I don't know Ali's e-mail address. _____

7. Mr. Jones is having a new job. _____

8. This cell phone doesn't belong to me. _____

# 1 Vocabulary and Language Workout

**A** Read the TV listing and fill in the blanks with words from the box. Be sure to use the correct form of the word.

prove

figure out

investigate

explain

mystery

theory

make sense

solve

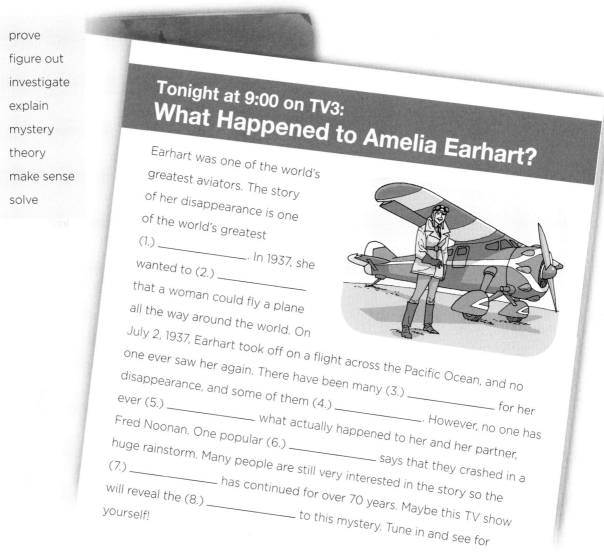

**Tonight at 9:00 on TV3:**
## What Happened to Amelia Earhart?

Earhart was one of the world's greatest aviators. The story of her disappearance is one of the world's greatest (1.) _____. In 1937, she wanted to (2.) _____ that a woman could fly a plane all the way around the world. On July 2, 1937, Earhart took off on a flight across the Pacific Ocean, and no one ever saw her again. There have been many (3.) _____ for her disappearance, and some of them (4.) _____. However, no one has ever (5.) _____ what actually happened to her and her partner, Fred Noonan. One popular (6.) _____ says that they crashed in a huge rainstorm. Many people are still very interested in the story so the (7.) _____ has continued for over 70 years. Maybe this TV show will reveal the (8.) _____ to this mystery. Tune in and see for yourself!

**B** You are relaxing in the park with friends. Suddenly you see a strange-looking object in the sky. Make five statements about the object. Use each of these modals once: *may, might, could, can't, couldn't.*

1. _____
2. _____
3. _____
4. _____
5. _____

# 2 Reading and Writing

**A** Read the article below and find the answers to these questions.

1. What happened? _____

2. Where did it happen? _____

3. When did it happen? _____

**B** Now read the article and think about what happened.

## The Tunguska Mystery

It was early morning, June 30, 1908, in eastern Russia. Suddenly, a terrible explosion rocked the forest in Tunguska. People fell to the ground, and all the trees for 2000 square kilometers were knocked down. People heard the explosion 800 kilometers away, and the fire burned for many weeks.

What caused this terrible explosion? A century later, scientists are still trying to find the answer. Here are some possible explanations:

1. **An asteroid:** Asteroids are large pieces of rock that go around in space and sometimes hit the planet. They can cause lots of damage. Some of them weigh as much as 100,000 tons. If an asteroid hit the earth, it would cause a huge explosion.

2. **A comet:** Comets are giant balls of gas, ice, and rock with long tails. They travel through space in a regular pattern. Encke's Comet was near Earth in 1908, and it's possible that a part of it broke off and hit the earth.

3. **A UFO accident:** Some people believe that a spaceship crashed into the ground in Siberia and its engine exploded.

4. **An extraterrestrial attack:** Another idea is that extraterrestrials (people from another planet) attacked the Earth.

5. **A science experiment:** Another idea is that scientists made a mistake during an experiment with electricity. A man named Nikola Tesla tried to build a "supergun" that used electricity. Maybe it was a test of his gun and it didn't work correctly.

**C** Write numbers in the boxes to match the pictures with the explanations in the reading.

 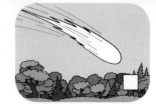

**D**   Complete the paragraph. Fill in the missing letters in the underlined words.

No one has ever been able to (1.) _e_____n_ what happened at Tunguska. There have been many different (2.) _i_____ns_, but there is still no clear (3.) _e_____n_. And how are we going to get (4.) _p_____f_ ? It happened over 100 years ago! Some of the explanations make (5.) _s_____e_ . But some of the (6.) _t_____s_ are just plain crazy. I have a feeling that this (7.) _m_____y_ may never be (8.) _s_____d_ .

**E**   What do you think? Write up your own explanation of the Tunguska mystery.

# 4 Today's Trends

## Lesson A Family trends

## 1 Vocabulary Workout

**A** Read and complete the charts.

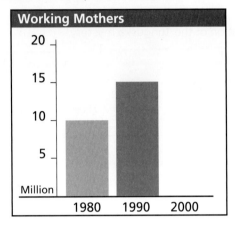

In our country, the number of mothers with jobs doubled between 1980 and 2000.

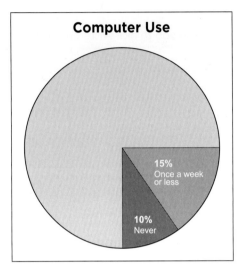

In this survey, fifty percent of teenagers say they use computers every day. Twenty-five percent use computers two or three times a week. Fifteen percent use computers once a week or less, and ten percent never use computers.

| Item | Before | Now |
|------|--------|-----|
| Newspaper | $1 | |
| Bed | $100 | |
| Car | $10,000 | |
| House | $100,000 | |

Prices in our country have increased very quickly. Since last year, the average price of a house has increased by twenty percent. Furniture is more expensive, too. The price of a bed has increased by twenty-five percent. The average price of a new car has increased by thirty percent. Even the newspaper costs more—the price has gone up by one hundred percent!

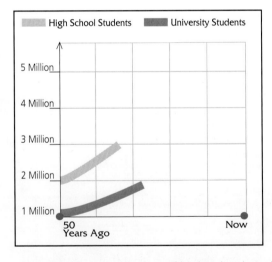

In our country, the number of high school students is twice as high as it was fifty years ago. The number of university students is three times as high.

**B** Write sentences about your country using these words. You don't need to use exact numbers.

1. over _____

2. increase _____

3. decrease _____

# 2 Conversation Workout

**A**   Match the sentence beginnings and endings to complete the expressions of disagreement.

1. I don't _____          a. true.
2. That's not _____       b. disagree.
3. Oh, _____              c. what you're saying, but . . .
4. I _____                d. come on!
5. I know _____           e. agree.

**B**   Read the statements and give your opinion and a reason. If you disagree, use one of the expressions from activity A.

**Example:**   Young people should get an apartment after they finish high school.
_I disagree. Some teenagers aren't ready to live alone at that age._

1. People shouldn't get married before they're 30 years old.

   _____

2. The best place for older people to live is with their children.

   _____

3. Mothers should not work outside the house.

   _____

4. People should live with their parents until they get married.

   _____

5. Small children should watch as much television as they want.

   _____

6. Couples with children should never get divorced.

   _____

7. Both boys and girls should help with the housework.

   _____

8. Day care is bad for children.

   _____

# 3 Language Workout

**A** Write about your friends. Use *all of, most of, a lot of, some of, a couple of,* and *none of*.

1. have a dog _____
2. like sports _____
3. send e-mail _____
4. are married _____
5. live near me _____
6. can drive _____

**B** Add quantity expressions to each sentence. Use *of* where necessary.

1. _____ Americans speak English. (most)
2. I know _____ the people on my street. (all)
3. We go shopping _____ times a month. (a couple)
4. _____ dogs can help blind people. (some)
5. _____ students study late at night before exams. (a lot)
6. _____ families have grandparents living with them. (many)
7. I finished reading _____ the books from the library. (some)
8. _____ my friends can come to the party on Saturday. (none)

**C** Write sentences about these houses. Use quantity expressions. Follow the example.

**Example:** *A couple of the houses have two doors.*

1. trees _____
2. white _____
3. flowers _____
4. three windows _____
5. very large _____

## Lesson B Fashion trends

# 1 Vocabulary and Language Workout

**A** Complete the sentences with words from the box.

| | | | |
|---|---|---|---|
| colorful | oversized | retro | unique |
| fitted | sporty | ripped | pointy |

1. Those shoes are so _____! I think they would hurt my feet.

2. She likes to play tennis and ride horses. She always wears _____ clothes.

3. She makes her own clothes so her dresses and blouses are _____.

4. I don't like pants that are sloppy and _____.

5. I like tight, _____ jeans.

6. She likes wearing her mother's clothes. They are so _____!

7. They often wear ugly old shirts that are _____ and dirty.

8. Some people wear only black, but Barry likes _____ clothing.

**B** Give advice to people about clothes and fashion. Use expressions from the box.

| could | should | ought to | had better not |
|---|---|---|---|

1. My friend's wedding is next week.

   _____

2. I'm really bored with my clothes, but I don't have any money to go shopping.

   _____

3. I have a job interview at a bank tomorrow.

   _____

4. I am going to visit your country in July.

   _____

5. I want to give my sister something cool for a birthday present.

   _____

6. I'm meeting my girlfriend's parents for the first time!

   _____

# 2  Reading and Writing

**A**  Read the article and the opinions below. Which opinions match which problems? Put the numbers in the correct spaces.

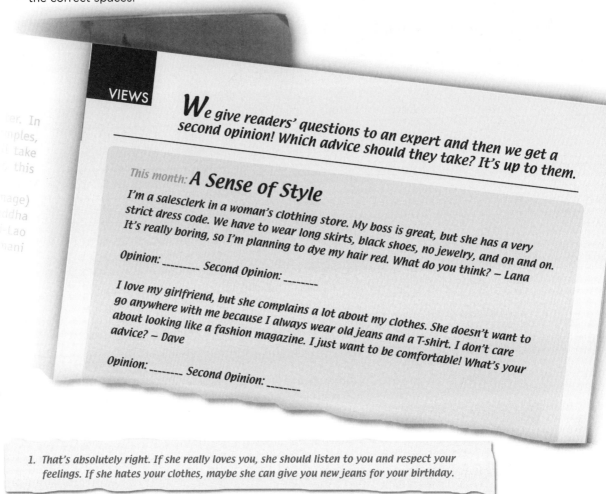

VIEWS

*We give readers' questions to an expert and then we get a second opinion! Which advice should they take? It's up to them.*

This month: **A Sense of Style**

I'm a salesclerk in a woman's clothing store. My boss is great, but she has a very strict dress code. We have to wear long skirts, black shoes, no jewelry, and on and on. It's really boring, so I'm planning to dye my hair red. What do you think? – Lana

Opinion: _____ Second Opinion: _____

I love my girlfriend, but she complains a lot about my clothes. She doesn't want to go anywhere with me because I always wear old jeans and a T-shirt. I don't care about looking like a fashion magazine. I just want to be comfortable! What's your advice? – Dave

Opinion: _____ Second Opinion: _____

---

1. *That's absolutely right. If she really loves you, she should listen to you and respect your feelings. If she hates your clothes, maybe she can give you new jeans for your birthday.*

---

2. *Sorry, but I have to side with your employer. A business wants to have a particular look, so they tell you what to wear. If you want to show off your individual style, you had better do it in your free time.*

---

3. *I disagree. Style is important because it shows our personality. Maybe you should find a new job.*

---

4. *I think you ought to have a serious talk with your girlfriend and explain how you feel. We all have our own style and taste. In my opinion, she thinks too much about appearances.*

---

**B**  Try to find the meaning of these terms from their context in the reading.

1. dress code _____

2. dye _____

3. complains _____

4. respect _____

5. side with _____

**C** Here's the next part of the article, "Second Opinion." Cross out the eight spelling mistakes and correct them on the lines below. The first one has been done for you.

All my friends have more money than I do, and they spend it all on shoping for clothings. I have to save money for my university expenses, and I can't afford to follow the trennds. My freinds never say anything about my sloply clothes, but I really wish I could look more uniqe. What should I do? — Cindy

Opinion: You should develope your own styleish look. Don't follow the crowd. Find your own look and you'll do just fine.

1. _shopping_     2. _____     3. _____     4. _____

5. _____     6. _____     7. _____     8. _____

**D** Now write a second opinion about Cindy's problem. Do you agree with the expert's opinion? Why or why not?

_Second opinion:_ _____

_____

_____

_____

_____

_____

_____

_____

_____

_____

## 1 Vocabulary Workout

**A** Use the words from the box to fill in the missing words in this list of errands.

| Go | Vacuum |
|----|--------|
| Mail | Do |
| Pick up | Take |
| Run | Make |
| Sweep | |

1. _____ grocery shopping.
2. _____ the mail at the post office.
3. _____ Aunt Clara's birthday present.
4. _____ the kitchen floor.
5. _____ the rug in the living room.
6. _____ the dishes.
7. _____ dinner.
8. _____ one final errand.
9. _____ a walk and relax.

**B** Think about yourself and your family. What errands do you usually do?

| Person | Errands |
|--------|---------|
| 1. You | |
| 2. _____ | |
| 3. _____ | |

# 2 Conversation Workout

**A** Number these sentences to make conversations.

1. _____ Could I come in next Friday?

   _____ Hello. Wagner College. May I help you?

   _____ Thanks. I'll be there for the 1:00 tour.

   _____ I'd like to make an appointment to tour the college.

   _____ We have tours on Wednesdays and Fridays.

   _____ Sure. There are tours at 1:00 and 3:00 in the afternoon.

2. _____ This is Fatma Aslan. I'm calling about seeing a language tutor.

   _____ English Department. This is Alan speaking.

   _____ I can help you with that.

   _____ How about 2:00?

   _____ Can I come in this afternoon?

   _____ That's perfect! Thanks.

3. _____ How's tomorrow at 3:00?

   _____ Professor Classon speaking.

   _____ That time isn't good for me. I have a class.

   _____ That works great. Thanks, Professor Classon.

   _____ This is Alma. I'm calling to reschedule our meeting.

   _____ Can you make it at 5:00 tomorrow?

# 3  Language Workout

**A**  Write a request for each situation. Use *can you, could you, will you, would you,* or *would you mind.*

1. You're at a job interview. You don't understand the question.

   _____

2. You're at a restaurant with your friends. You don't have enough money.

   _____

3. You're trying to study. Your brother is watching TV.

   _____

4. Your teacher is speaking very quietly. You can't hear.

   _____

5. You're cleaning your apartment with your roommate. The furniture is very heavy.

   _____

6. You're writing a paper in English. You think there are some mistakes.

   _____

7. Your friend is going shopping. You need some coffee.

   _____

8. You don't have time to cook dinner for the family. Your sister is talking on the phone.

   _____

**B**  Agree to these requests. Circle your answers.

1. Would you mind going to the store for me?

   *Yes, of course.*          *No, not at all.*

2. Would you drive me to my dentist appointment?

   *I'd be glad to.*          *Sorry, but I would.*

3. Can you help me with my errands?

   *Sure.*          *Not at all.*

4. Would you answer the phone, please?

   *OK.*          *No, I'd be glad to.*

**C**  There is one mistake in each sentence. Cross it out and rewrite the sentence correctly.

1. Could you mind turning off the radio? _____

2. Will you lending me your cell phone for a minute? _____

3. Could you closed the window, please? _____

4. Can you explaining that to me again? _____

5. Would you mind help me with this computer? _____

# 1 Vocabulary and Language Workout

**A** Look at the clue and then unscramble each word.

| | | |
|---|---|---|
| 1. drie | what you do on a bike | _____ |
| 2. letvar | go somewhere | _____ |
| 3. cuskt | not moving | _____ |
| 4. motucem | how you get to work | _____ |
| 5. hotsr | opposite of long | _____ |
| 6. ratin | something you can catch | _____ |
| 7. nedps | you can do it with time | _____ |
| 8. tale | not on time | _____ |

**B** Complete the sentences. Use a word from activity A.

1. Some of my friends _____ to jobs in other cities every day.

2. I usually catch the 9:00 _____ to Boston.

3. I like to _____ in the summer.

4. Do you ever _____ your bike to work?

5. My commute takes a _____ time—about ten minutes.

6. I'm running _____. I have to hurry.

7. This morning I was _____ in traffic for half an hour.

8. How much time do you _____ getting to school every day?

**C** Circle the correct words to complete each sentence.

1. I don't _____ like to take the subway.

   pretty          really

2. Hal has _____ long walk to school.

   pretty          a pretty

3. I don't have _____ nice car.

   very           a very

4. I can walk _____ fast.

   very           a very

5. She _____ enjoys riding her bike.

   really          pretty

6. The train has _____ comfortable seats.

   really          a really

# 2 Reading and Writing

**A** Look through this magazine article and circle all the modes of transportation. How many did you find? _____

## Better Transportation for Better Neighborhoods

Two South American cities are world leaders in transportation.

In the 1970s, Curitiba was one of Brazil's fastest growing cities, with serious pollution problems. The local government started several programs to reduce people's need for cars. World-famous innovations included new extra-large buses, special new roads for buses only, and a road system that keeps highways out of the city center. This plan has been very successful. Curitiba's population has grown by more than one hundred percent since 1974, but traffic has decreased by thirty percent. Curitiba has reduced air pollution and provided cleaner neighborhoods for its citizens.

Bogota, Colombia used different ideas. Many people there wanted to build a subway system, but subways are very expensive. Instead, the city built many new roads for bicycling and walking only. The government bought hundreds of buses. In 2002, the city celebrated Car-Free Day, and seven million citizens went to work without a car. And every Sunday, 125 kilometers of roads are closed to cars. Every weekend, up to two million people in Bogota come out to enjoy the clean air and quiet in their neighborhood.

Cities around the world can learn from these examples. Better transportation improves people's lives in many different ways.

**B** Now read the article again and complete the chart. Check the correct answers.

| Which city . . . ? | Curitiba | Bogota | Both | Neither |
|---|---|---|---|---|
| 1. has a new subway system? | | | | |
| 2. got new buses? | | | | |
| 3. built roads for pedestrians? | | | | |
| 4. improved their transportation system? | | | | |
| 5. reduced the number of cars in the city? | | | | |
| 6. built special new roads for buses only? | | | | |
| 7. got a new airport? | | | | |
| 8. closes some streets once a week? | | | | |

**C** Read this letter to the newspaper. Complete the letter with the correct form of a verb from the box.

| decrease | be | make | become | build | (not) let | solve | buy | increase |

Dear Editor,

Transportation (a) _____ a serious problem in our city. Every year people buy more cars, and the traffic (b) _____ more congested. We must do several things to (c) _____ this problem.

• (d) _____ a new train station downtown.
• (e) _____ the price of subway tickets.
• (f) _____ modern, comfortable buses.
• (g) _____ the tax on new cars.
• (h) _____ people park their cars downtown.

These ideas will (i) _____ our city a better place to live.

Sincerely,
Kim Mi-Ja

**D** Now write your own letter about transportation in your town or your neighborhood. Give as many ideas as you can.

## 1 Vocabulary Workout

**A** Solve this crossword puzzle.

**Across**

5. the noun form of *admit*
6. You have to _____ to a school in order to get in.
8. *Get accepted at* means *get* _____.
9. try hard to do better than other people

**Down**

1. make a _____ to do something
2. a form you complete when you ask to attend a school
3. what happens at the end of four years of college
4. the noun form of *compete*
7. Can you _____ a good dictionary for me?

## 2 Conversation Workout

**A** Match each sentence starter with the correct ending.

1. Look on _____          a. the other hand, it tastes good.

2. Yes, but on _____       b. this way.

3. Well, _____             c. then again, we don't have to pay for it.

4. Look at it _____        d. the bright side.

5. Yes, but _____          e. the good news is it's cheap.

**B** Number the sentences to make conversations.

1. _____ You're right. I guess I shouldn't be so upset.

   _____ Hi, Linda. What's happening with your college applications?

   _____ I'm disappointed. I didn't get into my favorite school, but I got into two others.

   _____ Well, look on the bright side. You got into two good schools.

2. _____ Seven. And they're all good schools.

   _____ I'm worried I won't get into a good college.

   _____ Well, the good news is you're sure to get into one of those schools.

   _____ How many schools did you apply to?

3. _____ That's strange.

   _____ I was hoping to have an answer this week.

   _____ I applied to five schools last month and I haven't heard anything.

   _____ Look at it this way. They have thousands of applications to look at and it takes a lot of time.

**C** Now write two conversations in which people offer a second point of view.
Use situations from your own life.

1. **A:** _____

   **B:** _____

   **A:** _____

   **B:** _____

2. **A:** _____

   **B:** _____

   **A:** _____

   **B:** _____

## 3 Language Workout

**A**  Write *A* or *B* to explain the reason for the underlined verb tense.

A. a decision made in the past          B. a sudden decision

1. I just heard the doorbell ring. <u>I'll answer</u> the door.                        _____

2. It's OK if you forgot your wallet. <u>We'll lend</u> you some money.       _____

3. <u>We're going to meet</u> in front of the library at 2:00.                        _____

4. <u>I'm going to go</u> to Oslo this summer.                                              _____

5. Luis <u>is going to use</u> his scholarship to study at Harvard.            _____

6. <u>I'll have</u> a chicken salad and iced tea, please.                               _____

**B**  Complete the sentences with the correct form of *will* or *be going to*. Use *be going to* for sudden decisions and *will* for plans that are already made.

1. I'm really hungry. I think I _____ make a sandwich.

2. I've already planned the menu. We _____ have Mexican food tonight.

3. We _____ visit our friends in Sydney in March.

4. It's really cold today. I think it _____ snow soon.

5. Your hands are full. You _____ drop that box.

6. On Friday, I _____ have dinner with Jeff at China Palace.

**C**  Your friend is making the following statements. Write a response to each one. Use *will* or *be going to*.

1. The phone's ringing.

   _____

2. I'm hungry.

   _____

3. I need a ride to the airport.

   _____

4. I'm thirsty.

   _____

## Lesson B After graduation

# 1 Vocabulary and Language Workout

**A** Number the expressions in the correct order, from soonest to latest.

_____ the week after next        _____ next week

_____ the day after tomorrow     ____1____ tomorrow

_____ next year                _____ in a few days

**B** Are these sentences about a definite time or an indefinite time? Write *D* for *definite* or *I* for *indefinite*.

1. _____ One of these days, I'm going to clean up my desk.

2. _____ Next week, I'm going to visit my grandparents.

3. _____ I'm going to be more careful about my diet in the future.

4. _____ In a few days, we're going to start taking tennis lessons.

5. _____ The day after tomorrow, we have a vocabulary test.

6. _____ Someday I'm going to travel all around Africa.

7. _____ Summer vacation starts the week after next.

8. _____ I'm going to start exercising every morning sometime soon.

**C** Look at the calendar. Today is July 1. Write sentences with *going to* and a time expression.

**Example:** July 9 / tennis with Carlos
       *I'm going to play tennis with Carlos next week.*

MONTH/JULY

| SUN | MON | TUE | WED | THU | FRI | SAT |
|-----|-----|-----|-----|-----|-----|-----|
|     |     | 1   | 2   | 3   | 4   | 5   |
| 6   | 7   | 8   | 9   | 10  | 11  | 12  |
| 13  | 14  | 15  | 16  | 17  | 18  | 19  |
| 20  | 21  | 22  | 23  | 24  | 25  | 26  |
| 27  | 28  | 29  | 30  | 31  |     |     |

1. July 2 / dinner with Angela

_____

2. July 18 / concert

_____

3. July 3 / English test

_____

4. July 5 / computer class

_____

5. July 11 / dentist

_____

## 2   Reading and Writing

**A**   Read this article from a student newspaper.

THE PAPER

# New Graduates Talk About the Future

After the City College graduation ceremony yesterday, we talked to three students about their plans and their dreams.

*Jameela Brown: I worked so hard for four years. I need a break now! I majored in biology and chemistry, and I had a summer job in a day-care center. I'm going to take a year off before I start medical school. My plan is to travel and do volunteer work in West Africa. I'll be a doctor someday, but I'm not sure what kind of doctor I'll be.*

*Jennie Min: I studied business, and it was easy for me to find a job. Next month I'll move to New York to start work at Giant Corporation. But I don't really want to spend my whole life working for a company. I hope I can start my own business. Maybe something with food. I love cooking! In college, I cooked dinner for my roommates every night.*

*Shane Peterson: Wow! Four years really went fast. I can't believe it's graduation day! My major was computer science, but I spent all my free time playing music. I played guitar in two different bands. I also play electronic music, using computers. I have job interviews with three software companies next week. I'm not worried about getting a job, but I really want to play music, too. That's my biggest dream.*

**B**   Complete this chart with information from the reading.

| Name | College Life | College Job / Hobby | Dreams | Plans |
|------|-------------|--------------------|--------|-------|
| Jameela | *major: biology and chemistry* | | | |
| Jennie | | | | - *move to New York*<br>- *work for Giant Corporation* |
| Shane | | | | |

**C**  Complete the sentences with the correct form of a verb in the box. Some of the sentences are predictions.

| work | become | get | start | have |
|------|--------|-----|-------|------|

I think Jameela (1.) _____ very interesting experiences in West Africa. She (2.) _____ in a day-care center. I think she (3.) _____ a doctor for children. I predict she (4.) _____ a job in a developing country, or maybe she (5.)_____ an organization to help sick children.

**D**  Choose another student in the article and write your predictions for him or her.

_____

_____

_____

_____

_____

_____

_____

_____

_____

_____

_____

_____

_____

_____

_____

_____

_____

_____

# Language Summaries

## Unit 1  All About Me

### Lesson A

**Vocabulary Link**

acquaintance
attend/go to (a school)
close friends
co-worker
date (someone)/go out (*with*
someone)
just friends
work together

**Speaking Strategy**

**Introducing a person to
someone else**

I'd like to introduce you to
    Andres.
I'd like you to meet Andres.

Junko, this is Ricardo.
Junko, meet Ricardo.
Junko, Ricardo.

**Responding to introductions**

It's (very) nice to meet you.
    (It's) nice/good to meet you,
    too.

Nice/Good to meet you.
    You, too.

### Lesson B

**Vocabulary Link**

get a good - bad grade
have (name of sport) practice
meet (*for* a time/*on* a day)
pass - fail (an exam/a class)
prepare (*for* something)
take a class
take a lesson
tutor

## Unit 2  Let's Eat!

### Lesson A

**Vocabulary Link**

delicious/tasty
fried
juicy
salty
spicy
sweet
tastes like

**Speaking Strategy**

**Making suggestions**

Let's have Thai food.
Why don't we have Thai food?
How/What about having Thai
    food?

**Responding to suggestions**

Great idea!
(That) sounds good (to me).
Fine with me.
I don't really want to.
I don't really feel like it.

### Lesson B

**Vocabulary Link**

a (balanced/healthy) diet
a (bad/unhealthy) habit
benefit
cut back (*on* something)
eat out
eliminate
increase
lifestyle
plenty (*of* something)
protect (*against* something)

# Unit 3 Unsolved Mysteries

## Lesson A

### Vocabulary Link

by accident - on purpose
good luck - bad luck
lucky/fortunately - unlucky
luckily - unfortunately
miss a chance - take a
   chance
reunite - separate
work out (for the best)

### Speaking Strategy

**Talking about possibility**

**Saying something is likely**

I bet (that) Marco plays drums.
Marco probably plays drums.
Maybe/Perhaps Marco plays
  drums.

**Saying something isn't likely**

I doubt (that) Marco plays drums.

## Lesson B

### Vocabulary Link

explain/explanation
figure out
investigate/investigation
make sense
mystery/mysterious
prove/proof
solve/solution
theory

# Unit 4 Today's Trends

## Lesson A

### Vocabulary Link

a quarter/one-fourth/
  twenty-five percent
almost/nearly
average
drop/decrease
half/fifty percent
over
percent
rise/increase
thousands
trend
twice/two times as high as
  (something else)

### Speaking Strategy

**Disagreeing**

**Politely**
I know what you're saying, but …
Sorry, but I disagree. / I don't
agree.
I hear you, but …

**Strongly**
That's not true.
I totally/completely disagree.
Oh, come on! / Are you serious?

## Lesson B

### Vocabulary Link

a look/style
**in** (style)/**out** (of style)

(body) piercings
baggy/oversized
casual
conservative
dramatic (hairstyle, makeup)
retro
ripped (clothes, jeans)
pointy (shoes, boots)
skinny/fitted (jeans)
sloppy
sporty

# Unit 5  Out and About

## Lesson A

### Vocabulary Link

do the chores
do the dishes
do the laundry
go grocery shopping
mail (something)
make a reservation
make an appointment
make dinner
pick up – drop off (something)
run an errand
sweep (the floor)
take (someone) to (a place)
take a break
take the dog for a walk
vacuum (a rug)

### Speaking Strategy

**Making appointments**

**Explaining why you're calling**
I'm calling to make a dental appointment.
I'd like to make a dental appointment.

**Scheduling the time**
Can you come in tomorrow at 2:00?
Can you make it tomorrow at 2:00?
How/What about tomorrow at 4:00?

> That's perfect. / That works great.
> No, that day/time isn't good for me.

## Lesson B

### Vocabulary Link

*ways to travel*
by bike, bus, car, plane, subway, taxi, train
on foot
catch/take a bus, cab, plane, subway, train
ride a bike

*talking about time*
*It takes* ... (+ time period)
a short time - a long time
(be) on time - (be) running late
pass (the) time (doing something)
spend time (*with* someone)

commute
stuck in traffic

# Unit 6  Student Life

## Lesson A

### Vocabulary Link

admit/admission
apply to (a school)/ application
apply for (something)/ application
compete/competition
decide/decision
get into/get accepted to (a school)
graduate/graduation
recommend/ recommendation

### Speaking Strategy

**Offering another point of view**

I didn't get into Yale.

> Look on the bright side …
> Well, the good news is …
> Look at it this way …
> Yes, but on the other hand …
> (Yes, but) then again …

> three other schools accepted you.

## Lesson B

### Vocabulary Link

*Definite time expressions*
**after** graduation/school/work
**in** two hours/days/months
**next** week/month/year
**this** summer/spring/fall/winter
the day after tomorrow

*Indefinite time expressions*
in a few days
in the near future
someday/one of these days
soon
sooner or later

# Grammar Notes

## Unit 1   All About Me

**Lesson A**   **Language Link:** The simple present vs. the present continuous

| | |
|---|---|
| I always **take** a shower in the morning.<br>The express train **arrives** at 9:03 a.m.<br>They **don't** **speak** Italian. They **speak** French. | Use the simple present to talk about habits, schedules, and facts. |
| Clara **isn't** **studying** <u>right now</u>.<br>She**'s talking** on the phone <u>at the moment</u>. | Use the present continuous to talk about actions that are happening at the time of speaking. Notice the <u>time expressions</u>. |
| How many classes **are** you **taking** <u>this term</u>?<br>Hiro **is living** in Singapore <u>these days</u>. | Also use the present continuous to talk about actions happening in the extended present (nowadays). Notice the <u>time expressions</u>. |

**Lesson B**   **Language Link:** Review of the simple past

| Subject | Verb | | Time expressions | |
|---|---|---|---|---|
| I<br>You | **missed**<br>**didn't miss** | | yesterday.<br>two days/weeks ago.<br>last week/month. | The past tense ending of regular verbs is -ed. For irregular verbs, see the list on the next page. |
| He/She<br>We<br>They | **had**<br>**didn't have** | a tennis lesson | | |

| | Yes / No questions | Answers |
|---|---|---|
| **With be** | Were you in class today? | Yes, I was./No, I wasn't. |
| **With other verbs** | Did you pass the test? | Yes, I did./No, I didn't. |

| | Wh- Questions | Answers |
|---|---|---|
| **With be** | Where were you last night? | (I was) at my friend's house. |
| **With other verbs** | When did you meet your girlfriend? | (We met) last year. |

| Regular past tense verbs | | | | Irregular past tense verbs | | | |
|---|---|---|---|---|---|---|---|
| Base form | Past tense | Base form | Past tense | Base form | Past tense | Base form | Past tense |
| change | changed | pass | passed | be | was/were | know | knew |
| die | died | play | played | come | came | make | made |
| enter | entered | prepare | prepared | do | did | meet | met |
| finish | finished | practice | practiced | eat | ate | read | read |
| graduate | graduated | study | studied | give | gave | run | ran |
| help | helped | talk | talked | get | got | take | took |
| live | lived | travel | traveled | go | went | think | thought |
| marry | married | use | used | have | had | win | won |
| move | moved | work | worked | keep | kept | write | wrote |

# Unit 2  Let's Eat!

**Lesson A**  **Language Link:** The comparative form of adjectives

| | |
|---|---|
| This restaurant is **bigger than** that one. | Use the comparative form of an adjective to compare two things. |
| Your cooking is **better than** my mom's. <br> My cold is **worse** today **than** it was yesterday. | The comparative of *good* is *better*. The comparative of *bad* is *worse*. |
| I'm tall, but Milo is **taller**. | Sometimes, you can use the comparative form without *than*. |

| | | |
|---|---|---|
| **One syllable** | sweet/sweet**er** | Add -*er* to many one-syllable adjectives. |
| | large/large**r** | Add -*r* if the adjective ends in -*e*. |
| | big/big**ger** | Double the final consonant and add -*er* if the adjective ends in a vowel + consonant. |
| **Two syllables** | simple/simple**r** <br> quiet/quiet**er** | Add -*r* or -*er* to two-syllable adjectives that end in an unstressed syllable. |
| | spicy/spic**ier** | Change the final -*y* to -*ier* if the adjective ends in -*y*. |
| | crowded/**more** crowded <br> famous/**more** famous | Add *more* to other adjectives, especially those ending in -*ing*, -*ed*, -*ious*, or -*ful*. |
| **Three syllables** | relaxing/**more** relaxing <br> delicious/**more** delicious | Add *more* to all adjectives with three or more syllables. |

## Lesson B  Language Link: The superlative form of adjectives

| | |
|---|---|
| It's **the oldest** restaurant in Paris. (= The other restaurants are not as old.) | Use the superlative form of an adjective to compare something to an entire group. |
| It's **one of the oldest** restaurants in Paris. (= It's one of many old restaurants in Paris.) | Use *one of …* to show that something or someone is part of a group. |
| Mario's has **the best** pizza in the city. It was **the worst** movie of the year. | The superlative of *good* is *the best*. The superlative of *bad* is *the worst*. |

| One syllable | sweet/**the** sweet**est** large/**the** large**st** | Add *the* and *-est* or *-st* to many one-syllable adjectives. |
|---|---|---|
| Two syllables | quiet/**the** quiet**est** simple/**the** simple**st** | Add *the* and *-est* or *-st* to two-syllable adjectives that end in an unstressed syllable. |
| | spicy/**the** spic**iest** | Add *the* and change the final *-y* to *-iest* if the adjective ends in *-y*. |
| | crowded/**the most** crowded famous/**the most** famous | Add *the most* to other adjectives, especially those ending in *-ing ,-ed*, *-ious*, or *-ful*. |
| Three syllables | relaxing/**the most** relaxing delicious/**the most** delicious | Add *the most* to all adjectives with three or more syllables. |

# Unit 3  Unsolved Mysteries

## Lesson A  Language Link: Stative verbs

| | |
|---|---|
| He **seems** like a nice person. Not:  ~~He is seeming like a nice person.~~ | Stative verbs describe states and feelings (not actions). Usually, they are not used in the present continuous. |
| I think he is dangerous. [think = believe] I am thinking about the problem. [think = consider] | Some stative verbs (for example, *have, feel, look, see, think*) can be used in the continuous. When used this way, their meaning changes. |
| She has a lot of money. [ have = own, possess] She's having coffee with a friend. [have = drink] | |

## Lesson B  Language Link: Modals of present possibility

| Subject | Modal | Main verb | | |
|---|---|---|---|---|
| Luis | **may** **might** **could** | be | sick. He's not in class today. | Use *may*, *might*, and *could* to say something is possible. |
| | **can't** **couldn't** | be | sick. I just saw him in the cafeteria. | Use *can't* or *couldn't* to say something is not possible. |

|  | Questions | Short answers |
|---|---|---|
| **With _be_** | Is Ian from the UK? | He might/could be.<br>He can't/couldn't be. |
| **With other verbs** | Does Marta have a brother? | She might/could.<br>She can't/couldn't. |

# Unit 4  Today's Trends

## Lesson A  Language Link: Quantity expressions

| With count nouns | | With noncount nouns | | Quantity expressions |
|---|---|---|---|---|
| 100% **All of** | | **All of** | | **Quantity expressions** are used to talk about amounts. |
| **Most of** | my friends live with their parents. | **Most of** | my homework is finished. | _a couple_ = two |
| **A lot of** | | **A lot of** | | Don't use _a couple_ (_of_) with noncount nouns. |
| **A couple of** | | _____ | | |
| 0% **None of** | | **None of** | | |

| General | **Most students** work hard. | [students everywhere] | _Most_, _some_, and _all_ can be used to make general statements about people or things everywhere. Notice the difference between the sentences in each pair. |
|---|---|---|---|
| Specific | **Most (of the) students** in my class work hard. | | |
| General | **Some families** have children. | [families everywhere] | |
| Specific | **Some (of the) families** in my neighborhood have children. | | |
| General | **All teachers** are strict. | [teachers everywhere] | |
| Specific | **All (of the) teachers** at my school are strict. | | |

## Lesson B  Language Link: Giving advice with _could_, _should_, _ought to_, and _had better_

| You **should/ought to** wear a suit to your job interview. | Use _should_ or _ought to_ to give advice. |
|---|---|
| You **shouldn't** wear jeans. They're too casual. | Use _shouldn't_ in the negative. |
| You **could** wear a suit to the interview. | Use _could_ to make a suggestion. It isn't as strong as _should_ or _ought to_. |
| You **could** wear your blue suit or the black one. | _Could_ is often used when there is more than one choice. |
| You**'d better** leave now or you'll miss your flight. | Use _had better_ (_not_) to give strong advice. It sounds like a warning. |
| We**'d better not** drive to the concert. It will be hard to park. | |

# Unit 5  Out and About

## Lesson A  Language Link: Polite requests with modal verbs and *mind*

| | Making requests | | | Responding to requests |
|---|---|---|---|---|
| informal | **Can/Will** you **Could/Would** you | help | me, please? | OK./Sure, no problem. / I'd be glad to./Certainly. / Of course. Sorry, but … |
| formal | **Would you mind** | helping | | No, not at all./No, I'd be glad to. Sorry, but … |

- Use *Can you, Will you, Could you,* or *Would you* + verb to make requests.
- To make a formal request, use *Would you mind* + verb+ *-ing*.
  Note: To agree to a *Would you mind* … request, answer with *No. (No, I don't mind.)*
- To make a request more polite, add *please*.

## Lesson B  Language Link: Intensifiers: *really, very, pretty*

| | | Adverb | Adjective | | *Really, very,* and *pretty* make adjectives and adverbs stronger. |
|---|---|---|---|---|---|
| I (don't) live | | really/very | close | to school. | *Really* and *very* are stronger than *pretty*. |
| I live | | pretty | | | |
| | | **Adverb** | **Adjective** | **Noun** | Only *really* or *very* can be used in the negative. |
| I (don't) have | a | really/very | long | commute. | |
| I have | | pretty | | | |
| | | **Adverb** | **Verb** | | *Really* can come before a verb. *Very* cannot. |
| I (don't) | | really | like | my new bike. | |

| I don't know John **at all**. (I've never met him.) I didn't like that movie **at all**. | You can use *at all* with negatives to mean *zero* or *never*. |
|---|---|

# Unit 6  Student Life

## Lesson A  Language Link: Plans and decisions with *be going to* and *will*

| Subject + *be* | *(not)* | *going to* | Verb | | Time expressions | Use *be going to* to talk about definite future plans (plans you have already made). |
|---|---|---|---|---|---|---|
| I'm<br>You're<br>He's/She's<br>We're<br>They're | not | going to | attend | Harvard | next month/year.<br>this fall.<br>in the summer.<br>after graduation. | |

---

**A:** What are your plans for today?
**B:** I don't know. Maybe I**'ll** <u>see</u> a movie.

**A:** Are you feeling OK?
**B:** No, not really. Maybe I **won't** <u>go</u> to class today.

Use *will* to talk about a sudden decision (one you make as you're speaking).

*Will* is followed by the <u>base form of a verb</u>.
*Won't = will not*

### Contractions

I'll = I will
you'll = you will
he'll = he will
she'll = she will
we'll = we will
they'll = they will

## Lesson B  Language Link: Predictions with *be going to* and *will*

| | |
|---|---|
| Leo gets all As. I'm sure he**'s going to**/he**'ll** get a scholarship to college.<br>She didn't study. I bet she **isn't going to**/she **won't** pass the test. | You can use *be going to* and *will* to make predictions about the future.<br>It's common to use *I'm sure* and *I bet* when you make a prediction you are certain about. |
| He'll probably get a scholarship to college.<br>She probably won't pass the test.<br>Maybe we'll find a cure for cancer someday. | You can use *probably* or *maybe* when you aren't 100% sure about your prediction.<br>*Probably* is stronger than *maybe*. |
| Look! That rock **is going to** fall. | Use *be going to* (not *will*) to make a prediction about an action that is about to happen very soon. |